CU00417543

Journal of Consciousnes

controversies in science & the humanities

Vol. 12, No. 6, June 2005

SPECIAL ISSUE: SHELDRAKE AND HIS CRITICS
The Sense Of Being Glared At

Edited by Anthony Freeman

Contributors

Rupert Sheldrake (*ars@dircon.co.uk*) is a biologist and a former Research Fellow of the Royal Society and Fellow of Clare College Cambridge. He has conducted independent research for the past 20 years and is author of several books includings *Dogs That Know When Their Owners Are Coming Home* (1999) and *The Sense of Being Stared At* (2003) .

Anthony Freeman (*anthony@imprint.co.uk*) is a priest in the Church of England, dismissed in 1994 for 'heretical' writing, since when he has been managing editor of the *Journal of Consciousness Studies*. His books include the volume *Consciousness: A Guide to the Debates* (2003) in the ABC-CLIO series 'Controversies in Science'.

Anthony Atkinson (*a.p.atkinson@durham.ac.uk*) completed BSc and MSc degrees in psychology at the University of Canterbury, New Zealand, and received a DPhil in Psychology (specializing in the philosophy of psychology) from the University of Oxford in 1997. He is now a lecturer in psychology at Durham University.

Ian S. Baker (*Ian.Baker@ed.ac.uk*) is a postgraduate researcher in the Koestler Parapsychology Unit, Edinburgh, currently completing the first PhD to research remote staring detection, examining the cortical electrophysiology involved in the processing of the phenomenon. He is also the Associate Editor of the *European Journal of Parapsychology*.

Susan Blackmore (*sblackmore@easynet.co.uk*) is a freelance writer, lecturer and broadcaster, and a Visiting Lecturer at the University of the West of England, Bristol. She has a degree in psychology and physiology from Oxford University and a PhD in parapsychology from the University of Surrey (1980). She no longer works on the paranormal. Her recent publications include the textbook *Consciousness: An Introduction* (2003).

William G. Braud (*william@integral-inquiry.com*) earned his PhD in experimental psychology at the University of Iowa in 1967. He has taught and conducted research at the University of Houston and the Mind Science Foundation (San Antonio, TX), and is currently Professor and Dissertation Director, Global Programs, Institute of Transpersonal Psychology (Palo Alto, CA), where he directs doctoral dissertation research, and continues research, teaching, and writing in areas of exceptional human experiences, consciousness studies, transpersonal studies, spirituality, and expanded research methods.

Published in the UK and USA by Imprint Academic, PO Box 200, Exeter EX5 5YX, UK
World Copyright © Imprint Academic, 2005. No part of any contribution may be reproduced in any form without permission, except for the quotation of brief passages in criticism and discussion. The opinions expressed in the articles and book reviews are not necessarily those of the editors or the publishers.

JCS is indexed and abstracted in: *Social Sciences Citation Index*®, *ISI Alerting Services* (includes *Research Alert*®), *Current Contents*®: *Social and Behavioral Sciences, Arts and Humanities Citation Index*®, *Current Contents*®: *Arts & Humanities Citation Index*®, *Social Scisearch*®, *PsycINFO*® and *The Philosopher's Index*.

Journal of Consciousness Studies ISSN 1355 8250   ISBN 1845400437
Cover Illustration courtesy of Melvyn Goodale

Jean E. Burns (*jeanbur@earthlink.net*) is a physicist who is interested in the relationship between consciousness and physical laws. She is a founder Associate Editor of the *Journal of Consciousness Studies* and was a co-editor of its special issue on parapsychology published in 2003.

Roger Carpenter (*rhsc1@cam.ac.uk*) is Reader in Oculomotor Physiology at the University of Cambridge. His main research interest is eye movements, and especially the neural decision mechanisms that determine where you look. He is the author of *Movements of the Eyes* and of the widely used textbook *Neurophysiology*. As far as consciousness is concerned he is a firm adherent of that deeply unfashionable belief, epiphenomenalism.

Chris Clarke (*chris.clarke@scispirit.com*) is Visiting Professor of Applied Mathematics at the University of Southampton. His books include *Living in Connection* (2003) the edited volume *Ways of Knowing: Science & Mysticism Today* (2005).

Ralph Ellis (*ralphellis@mindspring.com*) received his PhD in philosophy at Duquesne University with cross-disciplinary work in psychology, and a postdoctoral MS at Georgia State University. He teaches philosophy at Clark Atlanta University, and is co-editor of the annual book series *Consciousness and Emotion*.

David Fontana (*davidfontana@compuserve.com*) is Visiting Professor of Transpersonal Psychology at Liverpool John Moores University and author of over 20 books on various aspects of psychology. He is currently writing a major book on death and survival.

Christopher French (*c.french@gold.ac.uk*) is a Professor of Psychology and Head of the Anomalistic Psychology Research Unit at Goldsmiths, University of London. His research focuses on the psychology of paranormal beliefs and ostensibly paranormal experiences, and on the relationship between cognition and emotion.

Dean Radin (*dean@noetic.org*) is Senior Scientist at the Institute of Noetic Sciences and several times president of the Parapsychological Association. He is author of *The Conscious Universe* (1997).

Marilyn Schlitz (*marilyn@noetic.org*) is Director of Research at the Institute of Noetic Sciences and Senior Scientist at the Complementary Medicine Research Institute at the California Pacific Medical Center. She has published numerous articles on psi research and psychophysiology, cross cultural healing, consciousness studies and creativity. She has taught and conducted research at Stanford University, among other institutions.

Stefan Schmidt (*sschmidt@ukl.uni-freiburg.de*) is a psychologist and received his PhD from the University of Freiburg, Germany in 2002 with a thesis on distant intentionality experiments. He is currently a researcher at the Institute of Environmental Medicine and Hospital Epidemiology at the University Hospital Freiburg and also associated with the European Office of the Samueli Institute, Corona del Mar, Ca. He is currently conducting several parapsychological experiments (remote staring, telepathy, distant intention) and clinical studies (mindfulness meditation).

Max Velmans (*psa01mv@gold.ac.uk*) is a Professor of Psychology at Goldsmiths, University of London and is the author or editor of numerous books and papers on consciousness including *Understanding Consciousness* (2000), *Investigating Phenomenal Consciousness* (2000) and *How Could Conscious Experiences Affect Brains?* (2003). He is also science editor of the forthcoming *Blackwell Companion to Consciousness* (2006).

Anthony Freeman

The Sense of Being Glared At

What Is It Like to be a Heretic?

In September 1981 the prestigious scientific journal *Nature* carried an unsigned editorial (subsequently acknowledged to be by the journal's senior editor, John Maddox) titled 'A book for burning?' (Maddox, 1981). It reviewed and damned Rupert Sheldrake's then recently published book *A New Science of Life: The Hypothesis of Causative Formation* (Sheldrake, 1981) and raised a storm of controversy whose fall-out is still very much with us.

Up to this time Sheldrake was a well-respected up-and-coming plant physiologist and the recipient of academic honours including a fellowship at his Cambridge college. The furore that grew out of the assault in *Nature* put an end to his academic career and made him *persona non grata* in the scientific community. Over twenty years later this journal still runs the risk of ostracism by publishing his work. What can explain this deep and lasting antagonism?

The Origins of the Controversy

The saga began a week ahead of the book's publication, when Sheldrake had trailed his hypothesis of formative causation in an article in the *New Scientist* magazine. The piece was provocatively headlined: 'Scientific proof that science has got it all wrong'. An editorial introduction admitted that, to modern science, an idea such as Sheldrake's was 'completely scatty', but justified its publication on the grounds that first, 'Sheldrake is an excellent scientist; the proper, imaginative kind that in an earlier age discovered continents and mirrored the world in sonnets,' and secondly, 'the science in his ideas is good. ... This does not mean that it is right but that it is testable'.[1]

This was mid-June, and over the summer Sheldrake's ideas were subjected to much discussion in journals and newspapers, and his book was reviewed in a variety of scientific and religious publications. Attitudes were predictably mixed and by no means all negative. Then came the bombshell in *Nature*.

Nowhere did the editorial actually say the book under review ought to be burned. Indeed, it said the exact opposite: 'Books rightly command respect ... even bad

---

[1] Except where noted otherwise, the source of all direct quotations is the appendix of Sheldrake (1995).

Journal of Consciousness Studies, **12**, No. 6, 2005, pp. 4–9

books should not be burned; … [Dr Sheldrake's] book should not be burned.'
But it also contained the comment '[Sheldrake's] book is the best candidate for
burning there has been for many years' and — probably the real clincher — there
was that headline: 'A book for burning?' Dozens will read a headline who never
read the text, and how many of those troubled to note the question mark at the
end of the heading? Thus the myth was born: *Nature* says Sheldrake's book
should be burned.

What concerns us in this editorial is not Sheldrake's hypothesis,[2] but Maddox's 'hysterical attack' (as a writer to his own letters page called it a week or
two later). Why did the editor of *Nature*, himself a noted secularist, deliberately
invoke the language of book-burning, an activity inevitably associated not only
with religion, but with forcibly imposed dogmatic teaching? What caused him —
in the words of another correspondent — to treat his editorial column as 'a pulpit
from which to denounce scientific heresies'? The answer came most clearly in an
interview on BBC television many years later, in 1994, when Maddox said:

> Sheldrake is putting forward magic instead of science, and that can be condemned
> in exactly the language that the Pope used to condemn Galileo, and for the same rea-
> son. It is heresy.[3]

This quotation makes absolutely explicit a charge that appeared in more muted
form in the original editorial. Here Maddox had written that,

> Sheldrake's argument is an exercise in pseudo-science. … Many readers will be left
> with the impression that Sheldrake has succeeded in finding a place for magic
> within scientific discussion — and this, indeed, may have been a part of the objec-
> tive of writing such a book.

The image of Sheldrake as the opponent of science was also presented in a radio
discussion between the two protagonists in the autumn of 1981. In his closing
speech, Maddox first spelled out his very conservative approach to new theories:

> The conventional scientific view, which I think is entirely proper, is that there is no
> particular point in inventing theories which in themselves require a tremendous feat
> of imagination and constitute an assault on what we know about the physical world
> as it stands, when there is at least a chance, and in this case a good chance, in my
> opinion, that conventional theories will in due course provide an explanation.

After some further comments on the proper business of 'serious, sober scientists', he ended the programme — I sense more in sorrow than in anger — with
this lament:

> I am very worried indeed at the way that this will have comforted all kinds of anti-
> science people.

Several things in these quotations point to why Maddox found religious
terminology so appealing in his own defence of science, and they indicate how
similar in some respects are the scientific and religious establishments. These

---

[2] For a discussion of Sheldrake's hypothesis itself, in the context of his work on 'the sense of being
      stared at', see the commentary section of this special issue.

[3] Quoted from the transcript of a videotape of the interview in Dr Sheldrake's possession.

similarities throw light on the nature of the hostility most mainstream scientists and philosophers continue to show toward Rupert Sheldrake and his research programme.[4]

Heresy in Religion and Science

Sheldrake is accused both of 'putting forward magic instead of science' and of 'finding a place for magic within scientific discussion'. This is noteworthy because the only reference to book-burning in the New Testament is when the magicians of Ephesus, under the influence of St Paul's preaching, came out on to the streets and publicly burned their books of spells (Acts 19.19). There is an implied contrast here between the openly proclaimed teachings of Christianity and the secret arts of the magicians, and much early Christian polemic praised the transparency of the public orthodox tradition over against the secret knowledge claimed by the Gnostics. Orthodox science is orthodox religion's true heir in this respect, putting its trust in public replicable experiments rather than spooky unpredictable effects.

Another motif in the Ephesus incident is the idea that written words have an inherent power, so that false words need to be physically destroyed (burned).[5] In the debate over Sheldrake, this has its parallel in the view — expressed privately by a number of members of the *JCS* editorial advisory board, and in this volume by Christof Koch (this page) and Susan Blackmore (p. 64) — that his work should not be published in a reputable journal because 'bad ideas' will persist despite refutation. I discuss this proposition and explain the reasoning behind the publication of this symposium, in the following section.

---

[4] As illustrated by the following response from neurophysiologist Christof Koch to my invitation to join this symposium: 'I'll not comment on Sheldrake's papers because I think it is a waste of time. I would like to see hard physical, empirical evidence — and not just appeal to what Nobel laureate Murray Gell-Mann called quantum flapdoodle — for such a non-local mental "field" that would carry information from a subject in one room, observed via a video camera, to an observer at a remote location. Of course, this information would not have to interact specifically with any other subject who would then also claim to be stared at.

'Sheldrake has no understanding of modern neurobiology or modern theories of vision, confusing metaphors and museum exhibits with the ideas themselves — his characterization of how vision occurs in the brain is cartoonish.

'The morphogenetic fields postulated by Sheldrake to be necessary to explain developmental processes have proven to be equally elusive and molecular biology, coupled with the physical diffusion of various chemicals, has proven to be far more successful in explaining, in a predictive manner, how organisms develop from a single cell. Nor are such fields needed to explain animal communciation in non-vocal species. See, for example, the recent article by Couzin *et al.* (*Nature*, **433**, pp. 513–16, 2005) on how local mechanisms can explain rapid group decisions in animal collectives on the move (e.g. school of fish). No need for any spooky substances.

'Finally, I don't see how appealing to the beliefs of people makes a theory more or less true. In the US, far more people believe in ghosts, astrology, the literal truth of the bible and so on than in natural selection by evolution. That is a sociological but not an ontological observation.

'As a member of this journal's advisory board I'm surprised that *JCS* would give a platform to these sorts of ideas. It makes the job of those of us that seek to identify and study consciousness as a natural phenomenon, subject to known physical and biophysical principles, so much more difficult.' (Text of an email from Christof Koch to Anthony Freeman, February 10, 2005, reproduced here with the writer's permission.)

[5] Cf. Jeremiah 36, where the King burns the doom-laden prophecies of Jeremiah in an effort to prevent their fulfilment. The prophet responds by commanding his scribe to write them all out again.

A further point of interest is the choice of the term heresy. In a religious context, heresy is not simply false belief, it is a betrayal of true belief. An outsider may be in error, but only an insider can be a heretic. For early Christians, Judas was the father of heretics, because he was the follower of Christ who turned traitor. This sense of betrayal explains the vituperation that characterized writings against heresy, that was lacking in works directed at total non-believers (Wiles, 1967, pp. 29–30). Maddox regards Sheldrake as a heretic because he presents as science that which (in Maddox's eyes) is non-science, is magic. John Searle recently wrote 'that science does not name an ontological domain; it names rather a set of methods for finding out about anything at all that admits of systematic investigation' (Searle, 2004, p. 302). Sheldrake would agree with this and is trying to extend science as understood by Searle into realms it has hitherto eschewed. So anyone holding, *pace* Searle, that science is limited to a physical ontology will see Sheldrake as a traitor, and the stage had already been set for this by the *New Scientist* headline about 'scientific proof' that science was wrong.

I have personal experience of writing a religious book deemed to be heretical (Freeman, 1993/2001). It was not publicly burned, but did lead directly my dismissal by the Church of England and a hostile attitude from many former colleagues. Now, by associating with Sheldrake, I find myself experiencing again the kind of antagonism more familiar in the world of religion than science. The feeling in both cases is much the same — in parallel with Sheldrake's title *The Sense of Being Stared At*, we might call it the sense of being glared[6] at — and this has strengthened my view of the similarity between the two arenas.

Another clue to Maddox's motivation is his phrase 'anti-science people', which exemplifies the tendency to slice the world into 'goodies' and 'baddies', orthodox and heretic, pro-science and anti-science, 'us' and 'them'. This attitude grew out of a world view in which cosmic good and transcendental evil are in mortal combat at every level. Originating in the religion of ancient Mesopotamia and energized by Zoroastrian influences from the sixth century BC, it entered the mythologies of Judaism, Christianity and Islam and so became the 'master story' of western culture. We see it in all aspects of life from hero-touting movies, through popular literature, to the war against terror. But psychologist and theologian Harold Ellens shows in his introduction to *The Destructive Power of Religion* (2004) that this 'primal archetype of our understanding' is a huge mistake.

The consequences of this mistake are severe. There is no place in this narrative for ambiguous shades of grey, for the idea that humans are bound together by our common ignorance, seeking complementary paths to achieve our common goals. Instead there reigns a divisive moral dualism that breeds an assuredness of one's own correctness and the error of any who think otherwise. This leads inevitably to the heresy hunter's favourite dictum, that 'error has no rights'. Historically this has justified the burning not only of books deemed to be erroneous, but of their authors and readers as well. It is the same temper of mind that underlies

---

[6] The *Shorter Oxford English Dictionary* defines glaring (of the eyes) as 'staring fiercely and wildly'.

both John Maddox's assault on Rupert Sheldrake, with its allusion to book burning, and also the still apparent resistance to openly debating Sheldrake's ideas.

Controversies in Science and the Humanities

Given the situation described in the previous few pages, it was clear to me before I even read Rupert Sheldrake's submission that if I submitted it to peer review under the usual conditions, it would be rejected. Unless I deliberately picked unrepresentative referees (which would defeat the object of the exercise) some reviewer was bound to oppose publication on grounds that its whole approach undermined science (cf. Maddox's fear of giving comfort to 'anti-science people' and Koch's view that 'these sorts of ideas' should not be published because they impede the task of studying consciousness 'as a natural phenomenon, subject to known physical and biophysical principles'). To arrange for the submission to be rejected would have been the easy option, but would it have been appropriate for a journal that claims to publish 'controversies in science and the humanities'? I thought not.

An aspect of heresy (in its religious version) not so far mentioned is its association with what we now call 'paradigm shift'. St Thomas Aquinas, the greatest of mediaeval scholars and for centuries past the touchstone of Catholic orthodoxy, came in his lifetime within a whisker of being condemned for heresy (Chesterton, 1933). This was because the main thrust of his work was to reinterpret Christian doctrine into the then recently rediscovered philosophy of Aristotle. This shift from the neoplatonism in which the early Christians had forged their beliefs into new-fangled Aristotelian categories looked to many like the betrayal and destruction of the whole enterprise. At a level that is trivial by comparison, my own presentation of Christian teaching in the 'non-realist' or 'postmodern' categories was deemed by the Church authorities to constitute a betrayal and denial, rather than a translation, of traditional faith.

One way of looking at what Sheldrake is attempting is to treat it as a change of paradigm, from a science based in physicalism to an enterprise no less scientific that is open to a non-physical dimension. Maddox called this magic, and deemed it heresy, but there are less pejorative ways of describing it and many in the scientific consciousness community doubt that the physicalist paradigm will ever yield the full story. If the charge of heresy results from pushing at the boundaries, from seeking to enlarge the range of the investigation, then to suppress the work concerned seems at odds with the ideals of open public experimental science.

It was somewhat like the situation facing the editors some years ago over submissions to the parapsychology special issue of *JCS*. Had we held them to the same standards that apply in mainstream science, they would all have been rejected. Since the object of the exercise was to expose readers equally to parapsychologists' and sceptics' views of the field, and let them judge the merits of each side, such a result would have been self-defeating. So we agreed, on that one occasion, to allow certain assumptions and claims to stand that most in the scientific community would not accept, with the proviso that the parapsychologists were representing 'the mainstream views of their community reasonably well'. Critiques by other parapsychologists served as an appropriate form of quality control, in the circumstances. (See Freeman, 2003, for fuller discussion.)

In the present case I could not apply quite the same solution, because Rupert Sheldrake is a one-off and represents only himself. So the only alternative to outright rejection was to publish his work with open peer commentary to provide balance and criticism.[7] Such a procedure will never win the approval of those like Maddox and Koch, who in passages quoted above make clear not only their commitment to the existing paradigm but their opposition to exploring any alternative. But their viewpoint is not the only one found among the readers and editors of this journal. *JCS* exists to provide a meeting place for consciousness researchers with a wide range of backgrounds and working assumptions, as shown by the presence — from the very start — of names such as Huston Smith and Roger Walsh alongside those of Daniel Dennett and Bernard Baars on our editorial advisory board. The editors value and need this breadth of support in order to carry out the journal's unique role. The decision to proceed with this special issue was made in the knowledge that Sheldrake's work interests many of our readers and it reflects our commitment to open debate. It does not imply an endorsement of his ideas by the journal or any of its advisers.

The sense of being glared at — the awareness that one is the subject of distant and hostile attention — is undoubtedly an integral part of what it is like to be a 'heretic' whether in science or religion. It is an element in a wider and destructive sense of isolation, an isolation increased by the heretic's knowledge that he is 'dangerous to know' and therefore ought to discourage such friends as he does have from too open an association with him, for their own sakes. Believing as I am bound to do that those branded heretic are not always deserving of such treatment, I would like to see their isolating sense of being glared at transformed into a sense of being engaged with. Engagement, even in battle, holds the possibility of creative encounter, a positive outcome with potential value not only to the individuals but to the religious and scientific communities to which they belong.

The willingness of fourteen respected commentators to join this discussion of Rupert Sheldrake's papers and offer a variety of reflections — most of them a robust mixture of criticism and encouragement — leads me to hope that this is not an idle dream.

References

Chesterton, G.K. (1933), *St. Thomas Aquinas* (London).
Ellens, J.H. (ed. 2004), *The Destructive Power of Religion, Vol 1* (Westport, CT: Praeger).
Freeman, A. (1993), *God In Us* (London: SCM; 2nd ed. Exeter: Imprint Academic 2001)
Freeman, A. (2003), 'A long time coming', Editorial Introduction, *JCS*, **10** (6–7), pp. 1–5.
Maddox, J. (1981), 'A book for burning?', *Nature*, Editorial for 24th September.
Searle, John R. (2004), *Mind: A Brief Introduction* (Oxford: Oxford University Press).
Sheldrake, R. (1981/1995), *A New Science of Life* (Rochester, VT: Park Street Press).
Wiles, M. (1967), *The Making of Christian Doctrine* (Cambridge: Cambridge University Press).

---

[7] It has been pointed out to me that in *Behavioral and Brain Sciences*, which similarly publishes simultaneous commentaries, the target papers are still required to pass peer review first. I accept this, but for the reasons given, making successful blind peer review a condition of publication would in this case have killed the project at the outset.

Rupert Sheldrake

The Sense of Being Stared At

Part 1: Is it Real or Illusory?

I: The Sense of Being Stared At in People and Other Animals

Most people have had the experience of turning round feeling that someone is looking at them from behind, and finding that this is the case. Most people have also had the converse experience. They can sometimes make people turn around by staring at them. In surveys in Europe and North America, between 70% and 97% of the people questioned said they had had personal experiences of these kinds (Braud *et al.*, 1990; Sheldrake, 1994; Cottrell *et al.*, 1996).

The sense of being stared at is often alluded to in fiction, as in stories or novels by Tolstoy, Dostoyevsky, Anatole France, Victor Hugo, Aldous Huxley, D.H. Lawrence, John Cowper Powys, Thomas Mann, J.B. Priestley and many other writers (Poortman, 1959). Here is an example from Sir Arthur Conan Doyle, the creator of Sherlock Holmes:

> The man interests me as a psychological study. At breakfast this morning I suddenly had that vague feeling of uneasiness which overcomes some people when closely stared at, and, quickly looking up, I met his eyes bent upon me with an intensity which amounted to ferocity, though their expression instantly softened as he made some conventional remark upon the weather (Conan Doyle, 1884).

In questionnaire surveys about the details of these experiences I carried in Britain, Sweden and the United States, more women (81%) than men (74%) said they had felt they were being stared at. This experience occurred most commonly with strangers in public places, such as streets and bars. Also, significantly more women (88%) than men (71%) said they had found they could stare at others and make them turn around (Sheldrake, 2003a).

What emotions were involved when people turned round? For both men and women, curiosity was the most frequent reason for staring at others when they turned around, followed by a desire to attract the other person's attention. Less frequently, the motives were sexual attraction, or anger. Some people found that looking with distress, or affection, or good wishes could cause a person to turn

(Sheldrake, 2003a). In short, this sense seems to be associated with a wide range of motives and emotions.

Most people take these experiences for granted and pay little attention to them. But some people observe others for a living. The sense of being stared at is well known to many police officers, surveillance personnel and soldiers, as I have found through an extensive series of interviews. Most were convinced of the reality of this sense, and told stories about times when people they were watching seemed to know they were being observed, however well the observers were hidden (Sheldrake, 2003a). When detectives are trained to follow people, they are told not to stare at their backs any more than necessary, because otherwise the person might turn around, catch their eye and blow their cover.

According to experienced detectives, this sense also seems to work at a distance when the observers look through binoculars. Several celebrity photographers and army snipers told me that they were convinced that some people could tell when they were being looked at through telephoto lenses or telescopic sights.

In some of the oriental martial arts, students are trained to increase their sensitivity to being looked at from behind (Sheldrake, 2003a).

Many species of non-human animals also seem able to detect looks. Some pet owners claim that they can wake their sleeping dogs or cats by staring at them. Some hunters and wildlife photographers are convinced that animals can detect their gaze even when they are hidden and looking at animals through telescopic lenses or sights (Sheldrake, 2003a).

Conversely, some photographers and hunters say they have felt when they were being looked at by wild animals (Corbett, 1986; Sheldrake, 2003a). The early twentieth-century naturalist William Long described how, when sitting in the woods alone as a boy,

> I often found within myself an impression which I expressed in the words, 'Something is watching you.' Again and again, when nothing stirred in my sight, that curious warning would come; and almost invariably, on looking around, I would find some bird or fox or squirrel which had probably caught a slight motion of my head and had halted his roaming to creep near and watch me inquisitively (Long, 1919).

In a survey in Ohio, Gerald Winer and his colleagues at Ohio State University found that many people say they have sensed the looks of animals. In the Ohio survey, 34% of adults and 41% of children said that they had felt when animals were looking at them. About half the respondents believed that animals could feel their looks, even when the animals could not see their eyes (Cottrell, Winer and Smith, 1996).

If the sense of being stared at really exists, then it must have been subject to evolution by natural selection. How might it have evolved?

The most obvious possibility is that it evolved in the context of predator–prey relations. Prey animals that could detect when predators were looking at them would probably stand a better chance of surviving than those that could not (Sheldrake, 1999).

In spite of the widespread familiarity of this sense, until the late 1980s there was very little research on this subject, even by parapsychologists. I have been able to find only five reports of experimental investigations between 1885 and 1985, including two in unpublished student theses. The three most recent gave positive, statistically significant results.

Since the late 1980s, there has been an increase in research activity, which I review below. Most experiments have given positive, statistically significant results supporting the reality of this sense.

The main reason for the persistent neglect of this phenomenon has nothing to do with evidence or experience. It flows from a belief that the sense of being stared at is impossible.

II: Theoretical Reasons for Scepticism

There are two main reasons for the conventional dismissal of the sense of being stared at. First, it is classified as 'paranormal'. It is normal in the sense that most people have experienced it for themselves. But it falls foul of the general taboo against psychic phenomena. For generations, educated people have dismissed it as a superstition.

Second, it conflicts with the orthodox scientific theory of vision, first published in 1604 by Johannes Kepler (1571–1630), best known for his discoveries in astronomy. Kepler's was an 'intromission' theory, according to which light came into the eyes, but nothing went out of them. Vision was not in the outer world where it seemed to be, but inside the head.

Kepler's theory of the retinal image seemed to resolve a debate about the nature of vision that had been going on for two thousand years, and it was one of the first great triumphs of modern science. But his theory raised a problem that Kepler admitted he could not solve, and which is still unsolved today. The theory explained how images form on retinas, but it did not explain how we actually see. We do not see two tiny inverted images of the external world on our retinas. We see the world outside us, right way up, and single, not double. The only way Kepler could deal with this problem was by excluding it from optics (Lindberg, 1981). Once an object's images had formed on the retinas, it was someone else's business to explain how we actually see.

The mystery was relegated to the interior of the brain, where it has haunted science ever since. Ironically, the intromission theory left vision unexplained.

III: Scientific Investigations up to 1985

On Kepler's theory, the sense of being stared at ought not to exist. Hence it has generally been ignored by scientifically educated people, or dismissed as a superstition.

The first scientific paper on the sense of being stared at was published in *Science* in 1898 by E.B. Titchener, one of the founding fathers of experimental psychology in the United States. He found that many of his students at Cornell University firmly believed they could feel when they were being stared at from behind, or make others turn round by gazing at the backs of their necks. He was certain no mysterious influences could possibly be involved and proposed a 'rational explanation': people tend to turn round anyway; if by chance they see someone looking at them they remember it; if they do not, they forget it. Also, by turning round, their movement might attract the attention of someone behind them, so the two people might catch each other's eyes.

Titchener reported that he had carried out experiments on students' ability to detect stares and claimed they invariably gave 'a negative result; in other words the interpretation offered has been confirmed'. He published neither experimental details nor data. But he felt the need to justify doing the tests in the first place:

> If the scientific reader object that this result might have been foreseen, and that the experiments were, therefore, a waste of time, I can only reply that they seem to me to have their justification in the breaking-down of a superstition which has deep and widespread roots in the popular consciousness. No scientifically-minded psychologist believes in telepathy. At the same time, the disproof of it in a particular case may start a student upon the straight scientific path, and the time spent may thus be repaid to science a hundredfold.

Titchener's paper was very influential, and is still cited by sceptics today (e.g. Marks, 2003).

Another early American psychologist, J.E. Coover, was equally sceptical, but he was the first to publish methods and data (Coover, 1913). His experiments were carried out with his students at Stanford University. People worked in pairs; one was the subject, the other the looker. The subject sat with his back to the looker, who in a randomized series of trials either looked or did not look. In each trial, the subject guessed whether or not he was being looked at.

Coover claimed his results showed there was no significant ability to detect looks, and concluded that popular belief in the sense of being stared at was 'groundless'. By reinforcing Titchener's negative conclusions, Coover's work seemed to put an end to the matter from a scientific point of view, and apparently there were no more investigations in the English-speaking world for decades.

The next report in the scientific literature was in 1939, by J.J. Poortman, in Dutch. He published a summary of his paper in English twenty years later.

Poortman became interested in the subject as a result of his own experiences of being stared at, and through finding that many other people seemed to have experienced it too. Using a modified version of Coover's method, he carried out a series of trials with himself as the subject and a woman friend as the looker. She was a City Councillor in The Hague, and was accustomed to attracting the attention of other council members by the power of her gaze. Poortman was right significantly more often than wrong in guessing when she was looking at him (Poortman, 1959; statistical analysis in Sheldrake, 1994, ch. 4).

After Poortman's experiment, there was apparently no further research on this subject until 1978, when Donald Peterson carried out an experiment as a student project at the University of Edinburgh. The looker sat in a closed booth separated from the subject by a one-way mirror, and was invisible to the subject. The results were positive and statistically significant.

A few years later, Linda Williams a student at the University of Adelaide, Australia found a statistically significant effect when a person in a different room looked at the subject through closed circuit television (Williams, 1983).

IV: Recent Experiments with Direct Looking

Since the late 1980s, there has been an increase in research on the sense of being stared at, following two parallel approaches.

The first kind of experiment involves direct looking, using versions of the Coover procedure. People work in pairs, with a subject and a looker. In a randomized series of trials the subjects sit with their backs to the lookers, who either stare at the back of the subjects' necks, or look away and think of something else. A mechanical signal marks the beginning of each trial. The subjects guess quickly, in less than 10 seconds, whether they are being looked at or not. Their guesses are either right or wrong, and are recorded immediately. A test session usually consists of 20 trials, and takes less than 10 minutes.

In the second kind of experiment, the looker and subject are in different rooms connected through closed circuit television (CCTV), as discussed in the following section.

Direct-looking tests are far easier to perform than CCTV trials, and have now been carried out with many thousands of participants, both adults and children. Many tests have been conducted in schools. This research has been popularized through *New Scientist* magazine, BBC TV and Discovery Channel TV, and test procedures have been published on these organizations' web sites, as well as on my own (www.sheldrake.org), enabling numerous people to participate in this research. At least 20 student projects in schools and universities have involved staring experiments; several have won prizes at science fairs. Altogether, there have been tens of thousands of trials (Sheldrake, 2003a).

The results are remarkably consistent. Typically, about 55% of the guesses are right, as opposed to 50% expected by chance. Repeated over tens of thousands of trials this result becomes astronomically significant statistically (Table 1).

An alternative way of analysing the results, suggested to me by Nicholas Humphrey, is to use a 'sign' test, which gives an equal weighting to each subject. Those who are more right than wrong have a positive (+) sign, and those who are more wrong than right a negative (–) sign. For this analysis, all those equally right and wrong are ignored. By chance, the number of people with positive and negative signs should be the same. In fact (Table 1), 853 people were positive and 466 negative, a result very significantly above chance ($p = 1 \times 10^{-20}$).

In experiments in which the same subjects were tested repeatedly and given trial-by-trial feedback, there was a striking learning effect, with a significant ($p=0.003$) improvement in scores with practice (Colwell et al., 2000). In a German school, with repeated testing, some 8 to 9 year-old children achieved accuracies as high as 90% (Sheldrake, 1998).

Year	Trials	Right	% right	N	+	−	p
1998	3,240	1,843	56.8	160	97	42	3×10^{-6}
1999	13,903	7,636	54.9	661	387	186	1×10^{-15}
2000	4,800	2,544	53.0	294	150	94	.0002
2001a	8,060	4,385	54.4	403	197	134	.0003
2002	800	441	55.5	40	22	10	.03
Total	30,803	16,849	54.7	1,558	853	466	1×10^{-20}

Table 1. Results of direct staring experiments, expressed both as percentages of correct guesses and in terms of signs. Subjects who were more right that wrong were scored +, those who were more wrong than right, −. The total number of subjects is shown in the column N. The p values refer to the probability using the chi-squared test), with the null hypothesis that the number of + and − signs are equal. The year column gives the dates of my papers in which the results were published; thus, for example, 2000 refers to Sheldrake (2000).

This staring effect seems to be widely replicable. The data in Table 1 include the results from all 21 experiments of my own, in 20 of which the outcome was positive. They also include the results from 37 independent investigations in schools and colleges. Thirty-six of these investigations showed a positive effect, but one did not. I was notified of all these 37 investigations in advance, and have included all the data from them.

Dozens of other investigators have also taken part in this research and sent me their results, and again the great majority showed a positive effect. But because I was not notified in advance that these tests were taking place, I do not know whether there was a reporting bias: people who obtained positive results might have sent their data to me, while some of those that did not might not have sent them. Hence I have excluded all unsolicited data from the summaries in Table 1 because of this possible bias. Had unsolicited results been included, the overall significance of the positive effect would have been considerably higher.

Although most tests have shown the staring effect to be replicable, a few have not. Most notably, in a student project in the Psychology Department of the University of Amsterdam, in one out of three experiments, the results were at chance; in the other two, more subjects scored positively than negatively, but this effect was not statistically significant (Lobach and Bierman, 2004). But in these tests there were several differences in method from most other studies. Perhaps most importantly, in other investigations the subjects were blindfolded, whereas in this university study, subjects had to look at a computer screen throughout the tests, and to enter their guesses on the computer, which could have been distracting. In one experiment, they were also asked to evaluate their response to fragments of music during the tests, which could have provided an additional distraction.

Some of the studies conducted by sceptics have given statistically significant positive results, but others have been at chance levels, as discussed below.

In a student project in Ireland, Susan and Jennifer Brodigan compared the results with pairs of twins as lookers and starers with the results from pairs of untwinned siblings and people who were unrelated. In these trials, the subjects

were blindfolded and were not given feedback. The pairs of twins scored significantly higher than untwinned siblings or unrelated people (Sheldrake, 2001a).

The NeMo experiment

The largest experiment ever conducted on the sense of being stared at began in
1995 at the NeMo Science Centre in Amsterdam. By 2002, over 18,700 looker-
subject pairs had taken part, with positive results that were astronomically significant statistically (p = 10^{-376}, Sheldrake, 2003a).

In the NeMo Centre the test is presented as a question: 'Do you have eyes in
the back of the head?' The experiment is computerized. The subject sits about
two metres in front of the looker, with his or her back to the looker. For each trial
the looker is instructed whether to look or not by a signal on the computer screen,
in a random sequence provided by a random number program. The signal for the
beginning of each trial is given by a 'trrrrrr' tone lasting seven seconds, and the
end of which the subject know the trial has ended, and guesses out loud whether
he or she was being looked at or not. The looker enters the guess into the computer. Depending on the number of correct or incorrect guesses, after a maximum
of 29 trials, the computer announces whether the subject has 'eyes in the back of
the head' or not. This test is popular with children and their families.

The NeMo test was developed by Diana Issidorides, a cognitive psychologist,
and Jan van Bolhuis, a statistician at the Free University of Amsterdam. The
inbuilt statistical program is designed in such a way that if people guess at random, 20% would be classified as having 'eyes in the back of their head'. Against
this chance expectation of 20%, with data from 18,793 subjects, between 32 and
41%, depending on age and sex, had 'eyes in the back of their heads'. The most
successful subjects were boys under the age of 9 (Sheldrake, 2003a).

These tests were unsupervised, and there is no guarantee that some people did
not cheat. Because this possibility remains open, the results can only be taken as
an indication that test would be well worth carrying out under more controlled
conditions.

Online tests

A staring test has been running online on my web site (www.sheldrake.org) since
October 2002. Participants work in pairs, as usual, and do 20 trials in a randomized sequence, provided by a standard randomization program. When all 20 trials are completed, the computer gives participants a summary of their results and
all results are stored on a spreadsheet. By January 2005, 343 pairs had taken part.
The overall success rate was 61%. By the sign method, 232 subjects scored
above the chance level, and 70 below. These results were astronomically significant statistically. But again because the tests were unsupervised, there is no way
of assessing their reliability. Nevertheless, this online method makes it very easy
for anyone who anyone who wants to take part in this research to do so. Those
who suspect others of cheating or being influenced by subtle sensory clues can
carry out their own tests as rigorously as they like, or get their students to do them
under supervised conditions.

A

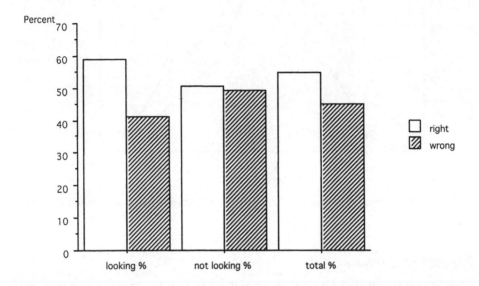

B

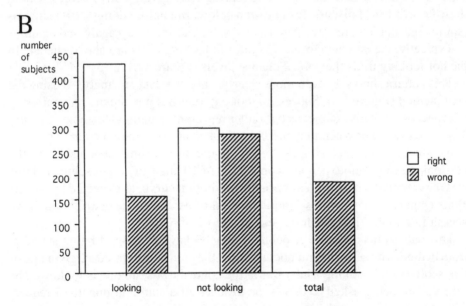

Figure 1. Combined results of experiments on the sense of being stared at carried out in Britain, Germany and the United States (data from Sheldrake, 1999, Table 5).

A (Above): The percentages of correct guesses in looking trials, not-looking trials and in total.

B (Below): The number of subjects who were more right than wrong compared with those who were more wrong than right in looking trials, not-looking trials and in total.

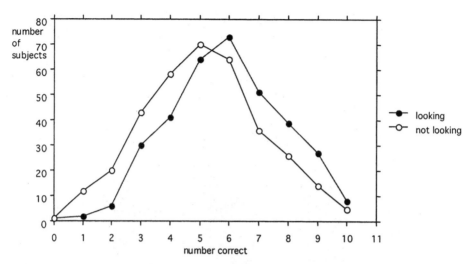

Figure 2. The distribution of scores in looking and not-looking trials in schools in Connecticut (Sheldrake, 1999).

The pattern of results

There is no doubt that most of these staring tests give positive scores. Could these be artifacts? I discuss this question below. But before doing so, it is important to consider a distinctive pattern of results that shows up again and again.

Typically, the percentage success rates in looking trials are above chance. In the not-looking trials they are at chance levels (Figure 1A).

This pattern shows up even more clearly when the data are analysed using the sign method (Figure 1B). Success in looking trials did not depend on a minority of especially sensitive subjects, but rather represents a general tendency for subjects to score better when they are being looked at than when they are not.

Another way of analysing the results points to the same conclusion. In the not-looking trials, more people scored 5 out of 10, than any other score, and this was the centre of a more or less normal distribution curve, as expected by chance alone (Figure 2). By contrast, in the looking trials, the entire distribution curve was shifted to the right, with its peak at a score of 6.

This pattern makes sense if people really do have a sense of being stared at from behind. The sense would operate when they are being stared at, giving positive scores in the looking trials. But in the control trials, no one is looking. The subjects are being asked to detect the *absence* of a stare, an unnatural request with no parallel in real-life conditions. Under these circumstances, subjects guess at random.

This characteristic pattern might imply that the results of the trials are not a result of cheating, subtle cues, implicit learning or errors in recording the data. These possible sources of error should have affected scores in *both* looking *and* not-looking trials, not just in looking trials.

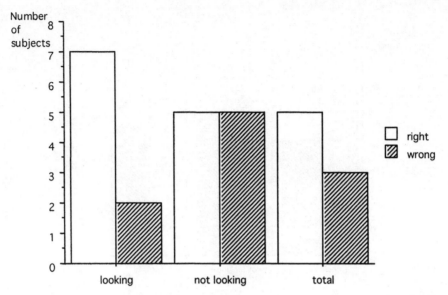

Figure 3. Results form the staring experiments of Coover (1913), showing the number of subjects who were more right than wrong compared with those who were more wrong than right.

However, as Schmidt (2001) has pointed out, there could be an alternative interpretation of this pattern. If subjects guess 'looking' more often than 'not looking', then by chance they will be more right than wrong in looking trials, and more wrong than right in not-looking trials. To take an extreme case, if a subject always said 'looking' she would be right in 100% of looking trials, and 0% in not-looking trials. The overall result would of course be at the chance level of 50%.

In a less extreme case, a 5% response bias in favour of saying 'looking' could give a pattern with 55% correct in looking trials and 45% in not-looking trials, again with a 50% overall.

Schmidt proposed that there was indeed an inbuilt response bias of 5% in favour of 'looking'. Hence by chance alone 55% of the guesses in looking trials and 45% of the guesses in not-looking trials would be correct. Now, if the subjects scored 5% above chance in *both* looking *and* not-looking trials, the overall result would be 60% correct in looking trials and 50% in not looking trials, with 55% success overall, as actually observed. Thus the characteristic pattern of results could be due to an underlying response bias of 5% in favour of guessing 'looking' together with a success rate 5% above chance in looking and not looking trials alike.

Both my own and Schmidt's interpretations fit the facts, and they cannot be distinguished from each other statistically (van Bolhuis, personal communication). However, Schmidt's interpretation depends on assuming that the response bias and success rate just happen to be the same, with the result that they cancel each other out in the not-looking trials. Schmidt also assumes that the response bias is the same in looking and not-looking trials. But this begs the question, because if the sense of being stared at is real, there will be a greater

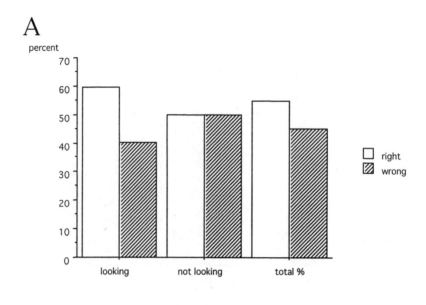

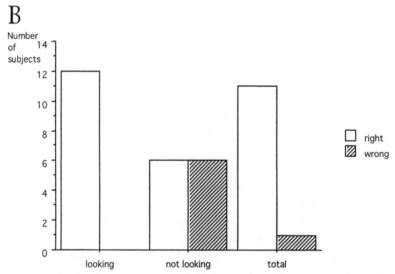

Figure 4. Results from the staring experiments of Colwell *et al.* plotted in the same way as in Figure 1. (Data from Table 1 of Colwell *et al.*, 2000, for trials in which subjects were given feedback.)

tendency for subjects to say they are being looked at when they really are, and so the 'response bias' will be greater in looking than in not-looking trials.

But however we choose to interpret it, this pattern of results is characteristic of direct-looking experiments. It even appears in the supposedly negative results of Coover (1913) when analysed by the sign method (Figure 3). This same pattern also appeared in an experiment that Colwell *et al.* (2000) carried out at Middlesex University, with the subjects and starers separated by a one-way mirror (Figure 4). A recent replication by Radin (2004) showed this same pattern again.

Possible artifacts

Perhaps one or more artifacts underlie these repeatable positive results. There are several possibilities:

1. *Subjects saw whether they were being stared at or not by peeping or peripheral vision.* This suggestion has been tested by blindfolding the subjects. Blindfolds made no significant difference (Sheldrake, 2001a). Also the positive results of Colwell *et al.* (2000) using a one-way mirror argue against this possibility (Figure 4).

2. *Subtle sensory cues.* When subjects and lookers were in the same room, perhaps the subjects could have heard sounds, picked up changes in infrared radiation or even detected different odours when the looker was staring or looking away. These possibilities were tested in experiments in which lookers and subjects were separated by closed windows and given no feedback. There was still a significant positive effect (Sheldrake, 2000). In addition, positive results in experiments using one-way mirrors and CCTV (described below) seem to eliminate the possibility of sensory clues.

3. *Cheating.* Separating lookers and subjects should have eliminated possible cheating. When they were separated by closed windows (Sheldrake, 2000), one-way mirrors (Fig. 4) or by closed circuit television, the results were still positive.

4. *Hand scoring errors.* In trials in which the lookers recorded the subjects' guesses by hand, there could have been errors in scoring. If these errors were non-random and biased in a positive direction, then the positive results could be a scoring artifact. In this case, the results should have fallen to chance levels when the subjects recorded their own guesses. Yet this did not happen; the scores were still positive (Sheldrake, 2000). The scores were also positive when subjects indicated their guesses by means of hand-held devices that recorded the results automatically (Colwell *et al.*, 2000; Radin, 2004). The data shown in Figure 4 were from automatically recorded trials. Also, there was no hand scoring in the CCTV trials, described below.

5. *Implicit learning.* In trials in which subjects are given feedback, they might learn to respond to subtle sensory clues or even to unintended patterns present in the trial randomizations. If so, these forms of learning should not take place when they are not given feedback. But subjects still scored very significantly above chance without feedback (Sheldrake, 1999, Tables 3 and 4; Sheldrake, 2000; Sheldrake 2001a, Tables 2 and 3).

The available data go against these artifact hypotheses.

Tests under 'real life' conditions

The kinds of experiments discussed above are very artificial. In experiments in more natural conditions, people are watched by hidden observers. Do they turn round more than when they are not being watched?

The lookers are hidden behind a one-way mirror or darkened window that overlooks a public space. Close to the lookers, a video camera films this public space continuously. In a randomized series of one-minute trials, the lookers either stare at the backs of people in this public space or do not look. Later, the videotape is evaluated blind by a person not otherwise involved in the experiment. This evaluator scores how many people turn around and look towards the camera in each one-minute period.

I carried an experiment of this kind at the BBC Television Centre in London in which the subjects (who had signed releases agreeing to be filmed by hidden cameras) were waiting to go into a studio as a quiz show audience. They had their backs to the hidden lookers, of whom I was one. There were six lookers altogether, including a member of the BBC Karate Club. We were invisible to the subjects because the office window was made of darkened glass and the lights in the office were switched off.

During the staring periods, we quite often saw people turn around and look straight towards us. The video was analysed independently by a judge who did not know which one-minute periods were staring periods and which were not. There were significantly more turns during the staring periods than during the not-staring periods: 27 as opposed to 12 (Sheldrake, 2003a).

The same experimental method can be used with non-human subjects, and has already been the basis of a student project in Italy, carried out in a bird park near Rome. Five students hid in bushes near a lake, from which they could watch resting geese on the shore through binoculars. The geese were filmed continuously. During the three-minute watching periods, each of the students observed a different goose, and in the three-minute non-watching periods they did not. An analysis of the video revealed that during the looking periods, on ten occasions geese woke up and looked towards the hidden observers, whereas in the not-looking periods this happened only three times (Sheldrake, 1996).

Very little research has so far been done under 'real life' conditions, but these preliminary experiments show that this experimental method is feasible with both people and animals.

V: Experiments Using Closed Circuit Television (CCTV)

Millions of CCTV cameras are used routinely for surveillance in shopping malls, banks, offices, airports, streets and other public spaces. My assistants and I have interviewed a representative sample of surveillance officers and security personnel whose job is to observe people through CCTV systems. We asked them about their experiences when watching people on the TV monitors. Most, but not all, were convinced that some people could tell when they were being watched, and gave examples to support this opinion (Sheldrake, 2003a). However, to be taken seriously, anecdotal evidence for the sense of being stared at through CCTV would need to be supported by evidence from controlled experiments.

Such experiments have already been performed. Starting in the 1980s, several parapsychologists have done tests using CCTV, with the subjects and lookers in separate rooms. In these tests the subjects were not asked to guess whether they were being looked at or not. Instead, their galvanic skin response was recorded automatically, as in lie-detector tests. In a randomized series of trials the lookers either looked at the subject's image on the TV monitor, or looked away and thought of something else.

Most of these experiments gave statistically significant positive results. The subjects' skin resistance changed when they were being looked at, even though they were unconscious of this change (Braud *et al.*, 1990; 1993a,b; Schlitz & LaBerge, 1994;1997; Schlitz & Braud, 1997; Delanoy, 2001). A recent meta-analysis of 15 CCTV staring studies confirmed that there was an overall statistically significant positive effect (Schmidt *et al.*, 2004).

VI: Sceptical Investigations

There are several campaigning organizations devoted to debunking 'claims of the paranormal', but the most active, prestigious and effective is CSICOP, the Committee for the Scientific Investigation of Claims of the Paranormal. CSICOP's publications include the *Skeptical Inquirer* magazine in the USA, and *The Skeptic* in Britain.

In response to the growing interest in the sense of being stared at, four CSICOP Fellows have recently investigated the phenomenon, namely Robert Baker, David Marks, Susan Blackmore and Richard Wiseman. So has Christopher French, the editor of *The Skeptic*. All five are academic psychologists. What have they found?

Robert Baker

Robert Baker, a retired professor of psychology at the University of Kentucky, made no secret of his preconceptions about the sense of being stared at: 'Skeptics ... believe that it is nothing more than a superstition and/or a response to subtle signals from the environment' (Baker, 2000, p. 40). He regarded his enquiries not so much as experiments but as 'demonstrations' of the non-existence of an ability to detect stares.

In his first demonstration, Baker selected people who were engrossed in eating or drinking, watching TV, working at computer terminals or reading in the University of Kentucky library. He unobtrusively positioned himself behind them and stared at them for an average of 8.6 minutes. He then introduced himself and asked them to fill in a response sheet. Thirty-five out of 40 people gave the expected response: 'During the last 5 minutes I was totally unaware that anyone was looking at me'. Contrary to Baker's prediction, two people reported that they had been aware that they were 'being observed and stared at' and three reported they felt something was 'wrong'. Baker noted that while he was staring at the subjects who felt something was wrong, 'All three stood up, looked around, shifted their position several times and appeared to be momentarily distracted on a number of occasions.'

Baker dismissed these unexpected findings. He argued that the three people who said something was wrong were not really affected by his staring, instead, he assumed that their restlessness was the *cause* of their feeling something was wrong. But this argument begs the question.

Baker also 'discarded' the results from the two people who said they knew they had been stared at. He regarded them as 'suspect' because one claimed he had extrasensory ability and the other claimed she was constantly being spied on (Baker, 2000). But if the sense of being stared at really exists, people who claim to have extrasensory abilities might be more sensitive than the average, and so might paranoid people (Sheldrake, 1994).

Baker then carried out a second demonstration in which he himself stared at subjects through a one-way mirror (Baker, 2000). The results were non-significant. But his experimental design was poor, and the instructions he gave to the subjects were ambiguous, confusing and self-contradictory (Sheldrake, 2001b; Baker, 2001).

David Marks

David Marks, a leading British sceptic, encouraged a fellow psychologist, John Colwell, to carry out a staring experiment in his laboratory at Middlesex University. Staring took place through a one-way mirror and Colwell and his colleagues tested the same subjects repeatedly. Subjects were given trial-by-trial feedback and improved with practice (Colwell *et al.*, 2000). The overall results were positive and very significant statistically, and showed a pattern similar to that in other tests (Figure 4).

In an article in the *Skeptical Inquirer*, Marks and Colwell (2000) tried to explain this unexpected result as an artifact of the randomization procedures. In their experiment, Colwell *et al.* (2000) used a set of 24 instruction sheets that were at that time provided on my web site. In response to a previous recommendation by sceptics (Wiseman and Smith, 1994), the randomization was counterbalanced on these particular sheets. Marks and Colwell speculated that rather than showing that people really can feel stares, their participants' positive scores arose from 'the detection and response to structure' present in this set of randomized sequences. But they offered no evidence that their participants did in fact learn to detect hidden structures in the randomization. By looking at the trial-by-trial scores, they could have seen if there really was an excess of successful guesses as a result of any structure they chose to postulate. When I offered to examine their data to test their hypothesis, they declined.

Even if subjects had learned implicitly to detect hidden structures in the randomization sequence, they should have improved in looking *and* not-looking trials. But this is not what happened. Scores improved only in the looking trials (Figure 4). Marks and Colwell did not mention this problem.

After their unexpectedly positive result, Colwell *et al.* (2000) did a second experiment using 'structureless' randomizations. This time the results were non-significant. They took this to confirm their implicit learning hypothesis. But in this second experiment there were two major differences, although Marks and Colwell did not mention this fact; the experiment was confounded. There was both a different randomization method and also a different looker, a colleague of Colwell's. When I raised the possibility of an experimenter effect (Sheldrake,

2001b), they dismissed it as 'a red herring' (Marks and Colwell, 2001). In fact experimenter effects are known to occur in staring tests, as discussed below.

Marks and Colwell (2001) entitled their *Skeptical Inquirer* article, 'The psychic staring effect: an artifact of pseudo randomization.' They claimed that my own results and those of other investigators were artifacts arising from the implicit learning of hidden patterns in this particular set of counterbalanced randomizations. But this hypothesis was contradicted by the facts. First, this set of randomizations was only used in some of my tests, and in many thousands of other tests there were different randomization methods. For example, in more than 5,000 trials the randomizations were provided by tossing coins, with highly significant positive scores (Sheldrake, 1999). Their prediction was also contradicted by results from over 18,000 subjects in the NeMo experiment, where the computerized randomizations were 'structureless'.

Second, the Marks and Colwell hypothesis predicted that the scores should be at chance levels in trials without feedback. But trials without feedback gave very significant positive results (Sheldrake, 2000).

Marks has strong beliefs and disbeliefs. He has quantified his disbelief in the sense of being stared as a probability of a million to one against (Marks, 2000). Two years after our exchange in the *Skeptical Inquirer*, he reiterated his original arguments in *The Skeptic* (Marks, 2003), omitting any mention of the evidence that went against his implicit learning hypothesis (Sheldrake, 2003b).

Susan Blackmore

A student of Susan Blackmore's, Jonathan Jones, carried out a CCTV staring experiment in 1996. His unpublished thesis was entitled 'Automatic Detection of Remote Observation and Schizotypal Personality Correlates'. His hypothesis was that people who scored highly on a Schizotypal Personality Questionnaire would be more sensitive to being stared at than those who scored low. According to the Abstract of his thesis, which he and Blackmore kindly sent me, this is what he found:

> As hypothesized, high scorers on the Schizotypal Personality Questionnaire were significantly aroused during stare trials compared to non-stare trials ($p=0.028$, 2-tailed) whereas low scorers were not ($p=0.313$, 2-tailed). This indicates the detection of Remote Observation by high Schizotypal Personality Questionnaire scorers.

Christopher French

Neal Rattee, a student of Christopher French's, carried out a CCTV staring experiment in French's laboratory in 1996. He found that there was a difference between subjects' responses in the looking and not-looking trials. Was this difference statistically significant at the conventional $p = 0.05$ level? No, according to a two-tailed combined t-test ($p = 0.096$). Yes, if a one-tailed test were used ($p = 0.048$). I asked Rattee and French if I could analyse their data using other statistical tests, but unfortunately this was not possible because they had discarded the data.

Richard Wiseman

In initial experiments using the CCTV method in Richard Wiseman's laboratory there was a statistically significant positive effect (Wiseman & Smith, 1994).

Wiseman and Smith then went back over their data to look for a possible flaw to account for this. They found that in their randomizations, more looking trials preceded not-looking trials than vice versa. They argued that this could have given rise to an artifactual positive result if subjects' galvanic skin resistance (GSR) declined throughout the session as they became more relaxed. They did not examine their data to see if this was in fact the case. They took it for granted that their hypothesis was correct.

I asked Wiseman if I could analyse the data to test their hypothesis. At first he told me that the results were inaccessible, but he finally managed to retrieve the data for 17 out of 30 subjects, which he kindly sent to me. I found that in ten cases GSR declined throughout the test session, while in seven it increased. The available facts did not support the Wiseman-Smith hypothesis.

In Wiseman and Smith's initial experiments, students served as starers. In subsequent CCTV experiments, Wiseman changed the procedure so that the experimenters themselves did all the looking. The results were then at chance levels (Wiseman *et al.*, 1995).

Could there be an experimenter expectancy effect when experimenters themselves serve as lookers? Experimenter expectancy effects are widely recognized in experimental psychology; experimenters tend to get results that confirm their expectations (Rosenthal, 1976), which is why many psychological experiments and clinical trials are carried out blind or double blind.

This possibility of an experimenter effect has been tested directly by Wiseman and Marilyn Schlitz, who jointly carried out a CCTV staring experiment in which half the subjects were tested with Schlitz as experimenter and looker, and half with Wiseman. As on previous occasions (Schlitz & LaBerge, 1994; 1997), Schlitz obtained significant positive results, while Wiseman's results were nonsignificant (Wiseman & Schlitz, 1997).

Such experimenter effects are not symmetrical. The detection of Schlitz's stares by the participants implies the existence of an unexplained sensitivity to stares. The failure of subjects to detect Wiseman's stares may imply only that Wiseman was an ineffective starer. He later said that he found staring 'an enormously boring experience' and that in most of the trials he was 'pretty passive about it' (Watt *et al.*, 2002).

Interestingly, the research initiated by all four CSICOP Fellows, Robert Baker, David Marks, Susan Blackmore and Richard Wiseman, gave positive results to start with. Baker, Marks and Wiseman then reacted to their positive findings in a similar way. First they tried to dismiss the results as artifacts. Then in follow-up experiments, they themselves, or their colleagues, did all the staring, achieving the non-significant results they expected.

By contrast, in the vast majority of tests by other investigators, the experimenters acted only as coordinators; the participants served as both starers and lookers. Under these conditions the results were overwhelmingly positive.

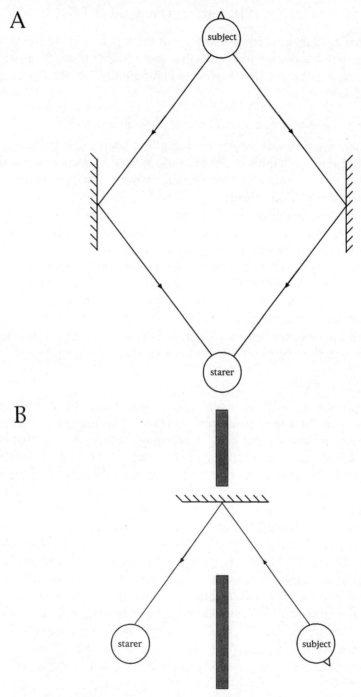

Figure 5. Diagrams showing the positions of starers and subjects in experiments involving mirrors, with rays indicating the reflection of light.

A (Above): The starer looks at the subject through a mirror on the left or on the right. The subject guesses which side the look is coming from.

B (Below): The starer looks at the back of the subject through a mirror in a doorway.

VII: Further Questions

Most of the available evidence implies that the sense of bring stared at is real. Given that the evidence is strong enough to merit further research, a series of new questions arise that can only be answered empirically. Some of these questions are as follows:

1. Does the sense of being stared at work through mirrors?

There is already much anecdotal evidence that people can tell when they are being stared at through mirrors, for example in bars. Many people say they have noticed that if they stare at someone through a mirror, that person may turn and look at them through the mirror.

My associates and I have carried out preliminary experiments on the effects of staring through mirrors using a variation on the usual procedure. Normally the starer sits behind the blindfolded subject, but in the mirror test, the subject sat in an adjacent room with the door open. The looker cannot see the subject's back directly, but only through a mirror positioned in the doorway (Figure 5B). The results were positive and statistically significant (Sheldrake, 2003a). This research needs to be repeated on a larger scale, and the effects of staring through mirrors need to be compared with the effects of direct staring. Is the effect just as strong through mirrors, or not? No one yet knows.

2. Is the sense of being stared at directional?

Most people who have felt they were being stared at say they have turned around and looked straight at the person staring at them. This implies that they detected the direction from which the look was coming, not just the fact that they were being stared at (Sheldrake, 2003a). People who have looked at others from upstairs windows often notice that the people not only turn round but also look up at them. Also people who have been stared at through mirrors usually say that they turn and meet the eyes of the person staring at them through the mirror, implying that they detect the direction of the reflected gaze.

This directional aspect can be tested by experiment. In one simple design, the looker sits behind the blindfolded subject. One mirror is placed on the looker's right and another on his left, in such a that he can see one side of the subject's head through one mirror, and the other side through the other (Figure 5B). In a randomized series of trials he looks at the subject through the mirror on the left or the right. The subject then guesses from which side she is being looked at, and raises an arm on that side to indicate her guess. In preliminary tests, I found that the guesses were correct significantly more than expected by chance (Sheldrake, 2003a).

3. Can people tell who is staring?

In real life, staring is often associated with emotions such as sexual desire and anger. For ethical and practical reasons it would be hard to test experimentally whether people can detect emotions associated with the staring. But it is possible to test whether they can detect something about the quality of the gaze by comparing different lookers. In trials with two different lookers, one or the other looks in a random sequence. Can subjects identify who is staring at them?

In order to avoid confounding different lookers with stares from different directions, both should stare from the same direction, with one sitting at a slightly higher level behind the other.

4. Does the sense of being stared at work on television?

If people can detect when they are being stared at on CCTV, what might happen if they are looked at on live television? Instead of one looker, as in the CCTV tests, there could be millions.

One possible design for a live TV test is as follows. Four experienced TV presenters sit is separate rooms in a TV studio, and all have cameras pointing at them and running continuously. Then in a series of randomized trials, one of these four people is shown to millions of viewers for a short period, say 5 seconds, and no one sees the others. At the end of each trial, all four subjects guess if they were being looked at or not, yes or no. In a series of trials, are the guesses at chance levels, or above chance? The subjects' skin resistance would also be monitored electrically, to pick up any unconscious physiological responses.

5. Can people tell when looks begin and end?

A general feature of the senses is that that they respond to changes and differences. Is this also true of the sense of being stared at? Is it easier for people to detect when someone starts or stops looking at them that to detect a constant stimulus or lack of stimulus?

6. Animal sensitivity

There is much to be learned about the sense of being stared at in animals. Can prey animals, such as mice, tell when predators, such as cats, are looking at them? What role does the sense of being stared at play in predator-prey relationships under field conditions? Does this sense work underwater, and are fish sensitive to looks? Are some animal species more sensitive than others? Can sleeping animals be woken by looks, as many pet owners claim?

VIII: Conclusions

Most people say they have sensed when they were being stared at, and most people also say they have made others turn around by looking at them. The sense of being stared at is taken for granted by most surveillance professionals, security officers, soldiers, celebrity photographers, martial arts practitioners and hunters. The ability to detect makes biological and evolutionary sense. It may be deeply rooted in our animal nature, and widespread in the animal kingdom.

The great majority of the evidence supports the reality of this sense. But there is still much that remains to be discovered, and more research is needed.

Fortunately, most of the experimental methods are inexpensive, and are very suitable for student projects.

If this sense really exists, it has major theoretical implications, which I discuss in the following article in this issue of the *Journal of Consciousness Studies*.

References

Baker, R. (2000), 'Can we tell when someone is staring at us from behind?', *Skeptical Inquirer* (March/April), pp. 34–40.

Baker, R. (2001), 'Robert Baker replies to Sheldrake', *Skeptical Inquirer* (March/April), p. 61.

Braud, W, Shafer, D. & Andrews, S. (1990), 'Electrodermal correlates of remote attention: Autonomic reactions to an unseen gaze', *Proceedings of Presented Papers, Parapsychology Association 33rd Annual Convention*, Chevy Chase, MD, pp. 14–28.

Braud, W, Shafer, D. & Andrews (1993a), 'Reactions to an unseen gaze (remote attention): A review, with new data on autonomic staring detection', *Journal of Parapsychology*, **57**, pp. 373–90.

Braud, W, Shafer, D. & Andrews (1993b), 'Further studies of autonomic detection of remote staring: Replications, new control procedures, and personality correlates',. *Journal of Parapsychology*, **57**, pp. 391-409.

Colwell, J, Schröder, S, & Sladen, D. (2000), 'The ability to detect unseen staring: A literature review and empirical tests', *British Journal of Psychology*, **91**, pp. 71–85.

Conan Doyle, A. (1884), 'J. Habakuk Jephson's statement', *Cornhill Magazine*, January.

Coover, J.E. (1913), '"The feeling of being stared at" — experimental', *American Journal of Psychology*, **24**, pp. 570–5.

Corbett, J. (1986), *Jim Corbett's India* (Oxford: Oxford University Press).

Cottrell, J.E., Winer, G.A. & Smith, M.C. (1996), 'Beliefs of children and adults about feeling stares of unseen others', *Developmental Psychology*, **32**, pp. 50–61.

Delanoy. D. (2001), 'Anomalous psychophysiological responses to remote cognition: The DMILS studies', *European Journal of Parapsychology*, **16**, pp. 30–41.

Lindberg, D.C. (1981), *Theories of Vision from Al-Kindi to Kepler* (Chicago: University of Chicago Press).

Lobach, E. & Bierman, D.J. (2004), 'The invisible gaze: Three attempts to replicate Sheldrake's staring effects', *Proceedings of Parapsychology Association Annual Convention, 2004* (in press).

Long, W.J. (1919), *How Animals Talk* (New York: Harper).

Marks, D. (2002), *The Psychology of the Psychic*, 2 ed. (Amherst, NY: Prometheus Books).

Marks, D. (2003), 'What are we to make of exceptional experience? Part 3: Unseen staring detection and ESP in pets', *The Skeptic*, **16**, pp. 8–12.

Marks, D. and Colwell, J. (2000), 'The psychic staring effect: An artifact of pseudo randomization', *Skeptical Inquirer* (September/October), pp. 41–9.

Marks, D. and Colwell, J. (2001), 'Fooling and falling into the sense of being stared at', *Skeptical Inquirer* (March/April), pp. 62–3.

Peterson, D.M. (1978), 'Through the looking glass: An investigation of the faculty of extra-sensory detection of being looked at', Unpublished MA thesis, University of Edinburgh.

Poortman, J.J. (1939), Het hegemonikon en zijn aandacht van den tweeden graad. *Tijdschrift voor Parapsychologie*, **11**, pp. 97–120 [In Dutch].

Poortman, J.J. (1959), 'The feeling of being stared at', *Journal of the Society for Psychical Research*, **40**, pp. 4–12.

Radin, D. (2004), 'The feeling of being stared at: An analysis and replication', *Journal of the Society for Psychical Research*, **68**, pp. 245–52.

Rosenthal, R. (1976), *Experimenter Effects in Behavioral Research* (New York: John Wiley).

Schlitz. M. & Braud, W. (1997), 'Distant intentionality and healing: Assessing the evidence', *Alternative Therapies*, **3**, pp. 62–73.

Schlitz, M. & LaBerge, S. (1994), 'Autonomic detection of remote observation: Two conceptual replications', *Proceedings of Presented Papers, Parapsychology Association 37th Annual Convention*, Amsterdam, pp. 352–60.

Schlitz, M. & LaBerge, S. (1997), 'Covert observation increases skin conductance in subjects unaware of when they are being observed: a replication', *Journal of Parapsychology*, **61**, pp. 185–95.

Schmidt, S. (2001), 'Empirische Testung der Theorie der morphischen Resonanz: Können wir entdecken wenn wir angeblikt werden?', *Forschende Komplentärmedizin*, **8**, pp. 48–50 [In German].

Schmidt, S., Schneider, R., Utts, J. and Walach, H. (2004), 'Distant intentionality and the feeling of being stared at: Two meta-analyses', *British Journal of Psychology*, **95**, pp. 235–47.

Sheldrake, R. (1994), *Seven Experiments that Could Change the World* (London: Fourth Estate).

Sheldrake, R. (1996), 'An experiment with birds', *Uccelli/Birds* (Zerynthia, Rome).

Sheldrake, R. (1998), 'The sense of being stared at: Experiments in schools', *Journal of the Society for Psychical Research*, **62**, pp. 311–23.

Sheldrake, R. (1999), 'The "sense of being stared at" confirmed by simple experiments', *Biology Forum*, **92**, pp. 53–76.

Sheldrake, R. (2000), 'The "sense of being stared at" does not depend on known sensory clues', *Biology Forum*, **93**, pp. 209–24.

Sheldrake, R. (2001a) Experiments on the sense of being stared at: The elimination of possible artifacts', *Journal of the Society for Psychical Research*, **65**, pp. 122–37.

Sheldrake, R. (2001b), 'Research on the sense of being stared at', *Skeptical Inquirer*, March/April, pp. 58–61.

Sheldrake, R. (2002), 'The sense of being stared at: An experiment at Holma College', *Gränsoverskridaren*, **10**, pp. 21–3.

Sheldrake, R. (2003a), *The Sense of Being Stared At, And Other Aspects of the Extended Mind* (London: Hutchinson).

Sheldrake, R. (2003b), 'The need for open-minded scepticism: A reply to David Marks', *The Skeptic*, **16**, pp. 8–13.

Titchener, E.B. (1898), 'The feeling of being stared at', *Science New Series*, **8**, pp. 895–7.

Watt, C., Wiseman, R. & Schlitz, M. (2002), 'Tacit information in remote staring research: The Wiseman-Schlitz interviews', *The Paranormal Review*, **24**, pp. 18–25.

Williams, L. (1983), 'Minimal cue perception of the regard of others; The feeling of being stared at', *Journal of Parapsychology*, **47**, pp. 59–60.

Wiseman, R. & Schlitz, M (1997), 'Experimenter effects and the remote detection of staring', *Journal of Parapsychology*, **61**, pp. 197–207.

Wiseman, R. & Smith, M. (1994), 'A further look at the detection of unseen gaze', *Proceedings of the Parapsychological Association 37th Annual Convention*, Parapsychological Association, pp. 465–78.

Wiseman, R., Smith, M.D., Freedman, D., Wasserman, T. & Hurst, C. (1995), 'Examining the remote staring effect: two further experiments', *Proceedings of Presented Papers, Parapsychology Association 38th Annual Convention*, Parapsychological Association, pp. 480–90.

Rupert Sheldrake

The Sense of Being Stared At

Part 2: Its Implications for Theories of Vision

For the purpose of this discussion, I am taking it for granted that the sense of being stared at is real. The weight of available evidence seems to support its factual existence, as discussed in my earlier article in this issue of the *Journal of Consciousness Studies*. Some people will dispute this conclusion, and there is as yet no universal consensus. But it is not necessary for everyone to agree that a phenomenon exists before discussing its possible implications. A discussion of the implications of evolution began long before everyone agreed that evolution had occurred, and there are still people who deny its reality.

The sense of being stared at implies that looking at a person or animal can affect that person or animal at a distance. An influence seems to pass from the observer to the observed. The sense of being stared at does not seem to fit in with theories that locate all perceptual activity inside the head. It seems more compatible with theories of vision that involve both inward and outward movements of influence.

In order to see the present situation in perspective, it is helpful to look at the history of the long-standing debate about the nature of vision. Inward or intromission theories have always tended to regard vision as passive, emphasizing the entry of light into the eye. Outward or extramission theories have always emphasized that vision is active. Combined theories accept that vision has both active and passive aspects.

I start with a brief overview of the history of theories of vision. I then discuss how this debate is continuing today, and examine how the different theories might relate to the sense of being stared at. I summarize my own hypothesis that the sense of being stared at depends on perceptual fields that link the perceiver to that which is perceived. These fields are rooted in the brain, but extend far beyond it. I conclude by examining aspects of quantum theory that imply two-way interconnections between observers and observed.

I: A Brief History of Theories of Vision

In the ancient world there was a long-running discussion about the nature of vision. This debate continued in the Arab world and in Europe in the Middle

Journal of Consciousness Studies, **12**, No. 6, 2005, pp. 32–49

Ages. For over two thousand years there were four main theories: the intromission theory, the extramission theory, theories combining intromission and extramission, and theories about the medium through which vision took place (Lindberg, 1981).

In ancient Greece, early in the fifth century BC, members of the Pythagorean School proposed an early version of extramission theory, suggesting that a visual current was projected outwards from the eye. Also, the philosopher Empedocles (c. 492–432 BC) proposed that the eyes sent out their own rays; they were like lanterns with their own internal light. Sight proceeded from the eyes to the object seen (Zajonc, 1993).

Meanwhile, the atomist philosopher Democritus (c. 460–371 BC) advocated an early version of the intromission theory. He was a prototypic materialist, propounding the doctrine that ultimate reality consists of particles of matter in motion. He proposed that material particles streamed off the surface of things in all directions; vision depended on these particles entering the eye. In order to account for coherent images, he supposed that the particles were joined together in thin films that travelled into the eye. The Roman atomist Lucretius (died c. 55 BC) called these films *simulacra*, and compared them to the smoke thrown off by burning wood, or the heat from fires, or the skins cast off by insects or snakes when they moult (Lindberg, 1981).

This intromission theory raised fundamental problems which proponents of rival theories delighted in pointing out. How can material simulacra pass through each other without interference? And how can the image of a large object like a mountain shrink enough to enter the pupil? This theory also failed to account for what happens once the films have entered the eye. How do they account for seeing? Intromission alone made vision into a passive process, and ignored the active role of attention.

Nevertheless, some atomists admitted that influences could move both ways, not just into the eyes, but also outwards from the looker. One reason for accepting outward-moving influences was the belief in the evil eye, whereby some people could allegedly harm others by looking at them with envy or other negative emotions. Democritus explained the evil eye as mediated by images moving outward from the eyes, charged with hostile mental contents, that 'remain persistently attached to the person victimized, and thus disturb and injure both body and mind' (Dodds, 1971). A belief in the power of envious gazes to bring about negative effects was common in the ancient world, and is still widespread in Greece and many other countries (Dundes, 1982).

The philosopher Plato (427–347 BC) adopted the idea of an outward-moving current, but proposed that it combined with light to form a 'single homogeneous body' stretching from the eye to the visible object. This extended medium was the instrument of visual power reaching out from the eye. Through it, influences from the visible object passed to the soul. In effect, Plato combined intromission and extramission theories with the idea of an intermediate medium between the object and the eye (Lindberg, 1981).

Aristotle (384–322 BC) followed Plato in emphasizing the importance of an intermediate medium between the eye and the object seen. but he rejected both the intromission and extramission theories. Nothing material passed in or out of the eye during vision. He called the intermediate medium the 'transparent'. He thought of light not as a material substance, but as a 'state of the transparent', resulting from the presence of a luminous body. The visible object was the source or cause a change in the transparent, through which influences were transmitted instantaneously to the soul of the observer (Lindberg, 1981).

The final major contribution of classical antiquity was that of the mathematicians, starting with the geometer Euclid (active around 300 BC). Euclid's approach was strictly mathematical and excluded practically all aspects of vision that could not be reduced to geometry. He adopted an extramission theory, and emphasized that vision was an active process, giving the example of looking for a pin, and at first not seeing it, but then finding it. There is a change in what is seen as a result of this active process of looking and finding, even though the light entering the eye remains the same (Zajonc, 1993). Euclid recognized that light played a part in vision, but he said very little about the way it was related to the visual rays projecting outwards from the eyes. He assumed that these rays travelled in straight lines, and he worked out geometrically how eyes projected the images we see outside ourselves. He also clearly stated the principles of mirror reflection, recognizing the equality of what we now call the angles of incidence and reflection, and he explained virtual images in terms of the movement of visual rays outwards from the eyes (Takahashi, 1992).

Other mathematicians, most notably by Claudius Ptolemy (active AD 127–148), took Euclid's geometrical approach further. Ptolemy proposed that the visual flux coming out of the eyes consisted of ether, or *quintessence*, or fifth element (over and above earth, air, fire and water). He rejected Euclid's idea of discrete rays coming out of the eyes with gaps between the rays, and thought of the visual cone as continuous.

The debate continued within the Arab world, especially between the ninth and thirteenth centuries AD. In Baghdad, Al-Kindi (c.801–c.866) helped start the debate in a new way. He saw the radiation of power or force as fundamental to all nature: 'It is manifest that everything in this world … produces rays in its own manner like a star. … Everything that has actual existence in the world of the elements emits rays in every direction which fill the whole world.' In an astonishing vision of interconnectedness, he thought that radiation bound the world into a vast network in which everything acted on everything else.

For Al-Kindi the laws of radiation were the laws of nature, and optics was fundamental to all other sciences. Under Euclid's influence, he thought of visual power issuing forth from the eye. Like Ptolemy, he did not accept the idea of distinct rays, but proposed that the visual cone was a continuous beam of radiation, sensitive throughout. He did not think of this radiation as an actual movement of material substance out of the eye, but rather as a transformation of the medium (Lindberg, 1981). Al-Kindi's treatise on vision became a popular textbook and influenced the course of thinking for centuries.

Alhazen (965–1039) put forward a new theory of vision that brought together ideas from the rival schools of thought into a new synthesis. He adopted the anatomical insights of Galen and his followers, the Aristotelian idea of a transparent medium, and the mathematical approach of Euclid and Al-Kindi. His principal innovation was to reverse the direction of the influences travelling in the visual cone. Instead of radiation moving out of the eye, light moved in. He thus laid one of the foundations for Kepler's theory of vision. But although his theory dealt impressively with the way that light entered the eye, he had much less to say about what occurred when it arrived there, and had no explanation of vision itself.

It was mainly through Arabic sources that these ideas were transmitted to medieval Europe, where astronomy and optics were the most flourishing sciences. Intellectual fashions changed as more material was translated. Up until the end of the twelfth century, the main influences were Platonic, and the extramission theory of vision was predominant. The influence of this theory increased when translations of Al-Kindi and Ptolemy became available, with their mathematical analysis of visual rays projecting out of the eye.

By the thirteenth century the works of Aristotle, together with the writings of his Arabic commentators, and the optical writings of Alhazen were part of a flood of new translations. Practically all the points of view and arguments from the classical and Islamic worlds were now available to European scholars in major centres of learning like Paris and Oxford.

In the Renaissance there was no radical break with the medieval theories of vision, but in four areas technological advances made major new contributions. First, there was the development of linear perspective in painting; second, an improved understanding of the anatomy of the eye, with a recognition that the lens is lens-shaped, when it was previously regarded as a sphere; third, the study of the *camera obscura*, in which inverted images formed on the wall of a darkened room with a small hole in the wall, as in a pinhole camera; fourth, the study of spectacle lenses, which led to the recognition that double convex lenses cause rays of light to converge (Lindberg, 1981).

All these advances provided essential ingredients for Kepler's theory of retinal images, published in 1604. His synthesis led to new problems, still unsolved today.

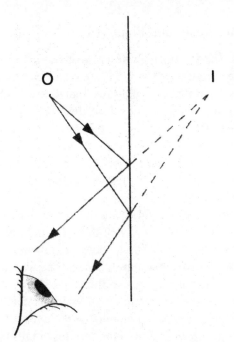

Figure 1. A typical textbook diagram showing how reflection in a plane mirror produces a virtual image (I) of the object (O). The dotted lines indicate virtual rays. (After Duncan and Kennett, 2001).

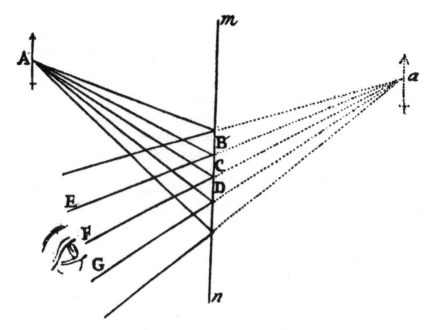

Figure 2. Isaac Newton's diagram of reflection in a plane mirror; 'If an Object A be seen by Reflexion of a Looking-glass *mn*, it shall appear, not in its proper place A, but behind the Glass at *a*.' (Newton, 1730, Figure 9).

II: Extramission Theories in Science and Popular Belief

Modern physics textbooks present an account of mirror reflections in which virtual images are produced outside the eye (Figure 1). The arrows on the light rays are of course shown as moving into the eye, but the 'virtual rays' that give rise to virtual images go in the opposite direction. This process is described as follows in a typical British textbook for 14-16 year olds: 'Rays from a point on the object are reflected at the mirror and appear to come from a point behind the mirror where the eye imagines the rays intersect when produced backwards' (Duncan and Kennett, 2001, p. 8). There is no discussion of how the eye 'imagines' rays intersecting, or how it produces them backwards.

Isaac Newton in his *Opticks*, first published in 1704, used the same kind of diagram (Figure 2). His very reasonable explanation was that the reflected rays incident on the spectator's eyes 'make the same Picture in the bottom of the Eyes as if they had come from the Object really placed at *a* without the Interposition of the Looking-glass; and all Vision is made according to the place and shape of that Picture' (Book I, Axiom VIII). But he does not discuss how vision is made from the pictures in the eyes, nor why images appear to be outside the eyes.

The theory of virtual images in Newton's *Opticks* and in modern textbooks is at least 2,300 years old. Euclid first codified the geometric principles of mirror reflections in his *Catoptrics*, and his diagrams showing the location of virtual images behind plane mirrors are essentially identical to those in modern textbooks (Takahashi, 1992).

Euclid's virtual images were formed by visual rays moving outwards in straight lines from the eye to the place where the object appeared to be. This theory of virtual images has survived continuously since time of Euclid because it works so well in explaining the facts of reflection and refraction. The virtual images are not explicitly ascribed to visual rays, but rather to rays 'produced backwards' from the eye.

Of course, supporters of the intromission theory say that diagrams of virtual images outside the eye should not to be taken literally. Contrary to what the text-book diagrams show, all images, real and virtual, are somehow inside the brain. Yet most science students are unaware of the complexities of consciousness studies, and probably believe what they are told. They are likely to conclude that vision somehow involves both the inward movement of light and the outward projection of images. Even before they are scientifically educated, most children believe this anyway.

In his study of children's intellectual development, Piaget (1973) found that children under the age of 10 or 11 thought vision involved an outward-moving influence from the eyes. Gerald Winer and his colleagues have confirmed Piaget's finding in a recent series of surveys in Ohio. Eighty per cent of the children in Grade 3 (aged 8–9) agreed that vision involved both the inward and outward movement of 'rays, energy or something else' (Cottrell and Winer, 1994). In the same age group, 75% said they could feel the stares of other people and 38% said they could feel an animal stare. There was a significant correlation between people's belief in the ability to feel stares and their belief that something goes out of the eyes when people are looking (Cottrell et al., 1996).

Winer and his colleagues were 'surprised — indeed shocked' by these findings (Winer and Cottrell, 1996, p. 138). They were especially surprised to find that belief in the ability to feel the looks of unseen others increased with age, with 92% of older children and adults answering 'yes' to the question 'Do you ever feel that someone is staring at you without actually seeing them look at you?' (Cottrell et al., 1996). They commented, 'the belief in the ability to feel stares, which occurs at a high level among children as well as adults, seems, if anything, to increase with age, as if irrationality were increasing rather than declining between childhood and adulthood!' (Winer and Cottrell, 1996, p. 139).

Winer and his colleagues also studied how beliefs in visual extramission changed with age. They were astonished to find that most adults believed in a combined intromission-extramission theory of vision, including college students who had been taught the 'correct' theory in psychology courses.

Our attention is now directed to understanding whether education can eradicate these odd, but seemingly powerful intuitions about perception... [A]s professionals and 'experts', we and many of our colleagues still find it difficult to accept the idea that college students could believe in visual extramission under almost any set of circumstances. In fact, a reviewer of one of our manuscripts commented that our work should be held to a higher standard of proof than other research is because evidence about extramission beliefs was so difficult for the reviewer to accept. It seems unusual, then, that education has produced a correct understanding for some of us, but has apparently failed to influence many children and adults in the same way (Winer and Cottrell, 1996, p. 142).

In further studies, Winer and his colleagues were yet more surprised to find that there was no decline in extramission beliefs among college students after studying the standard coursework on vision. They modified the teaching material to include explicit statements that in vision nothing leaves the eye, referring to fictional characters like Superman and the X-Men, portrayed with rays coming out of their eyes, stressing that in reality nothing like this happens. These refutational statements resulted in an immediate increase in the proportion of students giving the 'correct' answer. But to their disappointment this effect was short-lived, and the students soon reverted to a two-way theory of vision. They concluded, 'There is no doubt that psychology educators need to counteract a misconception that deals with one of the most fundamental areas of their discipline' (Winer et al., 2002).

III: Modern Theories of Vision

There is no agreement among philosophers, neuroscientists and psychologists about the nature of visual perception. Most take for granted the intromission theory, but others emphasize the active role of vision and its connection with bodily activity: vision is not confined to the inside of the head, but extends outwards into the world, closely linked to the organism's movements and actions.

It's all in the head

If all mental activity and all visual experience are confined to the insides of heads, then the sense of being stared at ought not to occur. And if it does, it is almost impossible to explain. This is probably why the phenomenon has been ignored for so long.

But there is no clear explanation of how vision actually occurs inside heads. In old-fashioned books of popular science, vision was illustrated through cutaway pictures of a man's head, inside which there was a miniature cinema, with a picture projected onto a kind screen inside the head, with a little person inside the brain looking at it (e.g. Kahn, 1949). Of course, this view results in an infinite regress, for in order to see this representation, the little person inside the brain would need a screen inside *his* brain, and a yet tinier person to see the screen, and so on.

The popular science approach still relies on this 'ghost in the machine' dualism. In the Natural History Museum in London, in 2005 there was still a ghostly display called 'Controlling Your Actions'. In a three-dimensional model of a man's head, a see-through plastic window in the forehead reveals the cockpit of a jet plane, with two empty chairs for the pilot and his co-pilot in the other hemisphere. The commentary explains, 'The cortex is the body's control room. It receives information, processes it and decides on the best course of action. So the cortex in your brain is rather like the flight deck of an aircraft'. Though carefully worded to avoid mentioning controllers or pilots, few visitors would expect a control room or a cockpit to make decisions without someone there to make them, even if the decider is invisible.

Since the 1980s, the predominant academic approach has been to suppose that vision depends on computational processing and on the formation of representations inside the brain. David Marr summarized this position as follows:

> Vision is the *process* of discovering from images what is present in the world, and where it is. Vision is therefore, first and foremost, an information-processing task, but we cannot think of it as just a process. For if we are capable of knowing what is where in the world, our brains must somehow be capable of *representing* this information — in all its profusion of color and form, beauty, motion and detail (Marr, 1982, p. 3)

Most of the metaphors of cognitive science are derived from computers, and the internal representation is now commonly conceived of as a 'virtual reality' display. As Jeffrey Gray put it succinctly, 'The "out there" of conscious experience isn't really out there at all; it's inside the head.' Our visual perceptions are a 'simulation' of the real world, a simulation that is 'made by, and exists within, the brain' (Gray, 2004, pp. 10, 25).

The idea that our visual experiences are simulations inside our heads is often taken for granted. But it leads to strange consequences, as Stephen Lehar has pointed out (Lehar, 2004). The simulation theory says that when I look at the sky, the sky I see is inside my head. This means that my skull must be beyond the sky! Lehar supposes that skulls are indeed beyond the sky:

> I propose that out beyond the farthest things you can perceive in all directions, i.e. above the dome of the sky, and below the solid earth under your feet, or beyond the walls and ceiling of the room you see around you, is located the inner surface of your true physical skull, beyond which is an unimaginably immense external world of which the world you see around you is merely a miniature internal replica. In other words, the head you have come to know as your own is not your true physical head, but only a miniature perceptual copy of your head in a perceptual copy of the world, all of which is contained within your real head (Lehar, 1999).

If all perceptual experience is indeed a miniature representation inside the brain, then looking at somebody from behind could not give rise to a sense of being stared at. This sense implies an ability to detect the focusing of attention by the person or animal that senses it. If attention is confined to the inside of the brain, it cannot act at a distance.

From this point of view, there are two ways to deal with the evidence for the sense of being stared at. The first is to deny or ignore it. The second is to accept it but to postulate a non-local mental effect whereby attention to someone's representation inside my brain influences that person at a distance by an unknown mechanism, perhaps akin to telepathy.

A grand illusion?

The theory that there is a detailed representation of the external world within the brain is by no means universally believed within academic circles. It is under attack by sceptical neuroscientists and philosophers.

The more that is known about the eyes and the brain, the less likely the internal representation theory seems. The resolving power of the eyes is limited, especially outside the foveal region; each eye has a blind spot of which we remain unaware; the eyes are in frequent motion, saccading from point to point in the visual field three to four times a second; and recent work on 'change blindness' and 'inattentional blindness' shows that we often remain unaware of large changes in the visual field. As Alva Noë has summarized the problem, 'How, on the basis of the fragmented and discontinuous information, are we able to enjoy the impression of seamless consciousness of an environment that is detailed, continuous, complex and high resolution?' (Noë, 2002). Is the visual world a grand illusion?

The most radical solution to this problem is to suppose that the visual world is not an illusion, and is not inside the brain at all. The visual world is where it seems to be, in the external world. The leading proponent of this view was J.J. Gibson (1979) in his 'ecological' approach to perception. Rather than the brain building up an internal model of the environment, vision involves the whole animal and is concerned with the guidance of action.

For Gibson, perception is active and direct. The animal moves its eyes, head and body, and it moves through the environment. Visual perception is not a series of static snapshots, but a dynamic visual flow. Because perceivers are familiar with regular correlations between this flow and the visual properties of the environment, they are able to 'pick up' information from the environment by 'direct perception'. As Gibson put it, 'Information is conceived as available in the ambient energy flux, not as signals in a bundle of nerve fibers. It is information about both the persisting and the changing features of the environment together. Moreover, information about the observer and his movements is available, so that self-awareness accompanies perceptual awareness' (Gibson, 1979).

Gibson's approach was of course much criticized, not least because it appears to contradict every aspect of the representational-computational orthodoxy (Fodor and Pylyshyn, 1981). Nevertheless, the problems posed by the internal representation theory have not gone away. Some researchers disagree with Gibson's theory of direct perception, but agree with him about the importance of movement and activity in perception.

In the 'enactive' or 'embodied' approach developed by Francisco Varela and his colleagues, perceptions are not represented in a world-model inside the head, but are enacted or 'brought forth' as a result of the interaction of the organism and its environment. '[P]erception and action have evolved together ... perception is always *perceptually guided activity*' (Thompson *et al.*, 1992).

O'Regan (1992) likewise rejects the need for internal representations of the world; the world can be used as an external memory, or as its own model. We can look again if we need to; we do not need a detailed model of the environment inside our brains. As Noë (2002) has summarized it, 'The enactive, sensorimotor account explains how it can be that we enjoy an experience of worldly detail which is not represented in our brains. The detail is present — the perceptual world is present — in the sense that we have a special kind of access to the details, an access controlled by patterns of sensorimotor dependence with which we are familiar. The visual world is not a grand illusion.'

It is not clear how these various approaches might relate to the sense of being stared at. Gibson's ecological theory places perceptual activity outside the brain, and hence leaves open the possibility of an interaction between the perceiver and the perceived. The same might be true of the enactive and sensorimotor accounts in that they are interactive by nature, and do not treat vision only as an internal process within the brain.

Two-way theories

In two-way theories of vision, images are projected out beyond the brain to the places where they appear to be. Thus if I look at a tree, light from the tree enters my eyes, inverted images form on my retinas, and changes occur in my eyes and in various regions of the brain. These give rise to a perceptual image of the tree, which is situated where the tree actually is. The tree that I am seeing is in my mind, but not inside my brain.

This theory of vision resembles the combined intromission-extramission theory widespread in ancient Greece, the Arab world and medieval Europe (Lindberg, 1981). Several recent philosophers have also advocated versions of a two-way theory, including Henri Bergson (1896), William James (1904), Alfred North Whitehead (1925) and Bertrand Russell (1948).

Bergson anticipated the enactive and sensorimotor approaches in emphasizing that perception is directed towards action. Through perception, 'The objects which surround my body reflect its possible action upon them' (Bergson, 1911, p. 7). He rejected the idea that images were formed inside the brain:

> The truth is that the point P, the rays which it emits, the retina and the nervous elements affected, form a single whole; that the luminous point P is a part of this whole; and that it is really in P, and not elsewhere, that the image of P is formed and perceived (Bergson, 1911, pp. 37–8).

William James likewise rejected the idea of images inside the brain. He took as an example the reader sitting in a room, reading a book:

> [T]he whole philosophy of perception from Democritus' time downwards has been just one long wrangle over the paradox that what is evidently one reality should be in two places at once, both in outer space and in a person's mind. 'Representative' theories of perception avoid the logical paradox, but on the other had they violate the reader's sense of life which knows no intervening mental image but seems to see the room and the book immediately as they physically exist (James, 1904; quoted in Velmans 2000).

As Whitehead expressed it, 'sensations are projected by the mind so as to clothe appropriate bodies in external nature' (Whitehead, 1925, p. 54).

Max Velmans currently argues in favour of a theory of this kind as part of his 'reflexive' model of consciousness (Velmans, 2000). He discusses the example of a subject S looking at a cat as follows:

According to reductionists there seems to be a phenomenal cat 'in S's mind', but this is really nothing more than a state of her brain. According to the reflexive model, while S is gazing at the cat, her only visual experience of the cat is the cat she sees out in the world. If she is asked to point to this phenomenal cat (her 'cat experience'), she should point not to her brain but to the cat as perceived, out in space beyond the body surface (Velmans, 2000, p. 109).[1]

How could this projection possibly work? He discusses the process as follows:

I assume that the brain constructs a 'representation' or 'mental model' of what is happening, based on the input from the initiating stimulus, expectations, traces of prior, related stimuli stored in long-term memory, and so on.... Visual representations of a cat, for example, include encoding for shape, location and extension, movement, surface texture, colour, and so on.... Let me illustrate with a simple analogy. Let us suppose that the information encoded in the subject's brain is formed into a kind of neural 'projection hologram'. A projection hologram has the interesting quality that the three-dimensional image it encodes is perceived to be out in space, in *front* of its two-dimensional surface (Velmans, 2000, pp. 113-4).

Velmans makes it clear that the idea of holographic projection is only an analogy, and stresses that he thinks perceptual projection is subjective and non-physical, occurring only in phenomenal as opposed to physical space. Nevertheless, these projections extend beyond the skull and generally coincide with physical space.

If these projections are entirely non-physical, it is hard to conceive how they could influence people or animals at a distance, or have any other measurable effects. Velmans' hypothesis does not seem to make any testable predictions, and in its present form would not provide a basis for the sense of being stared at. However, if one person's perceptual projections interacted with another's then the sense of being stared at would be consistent with this projection theory.

IV: Perceptual Fields

My own hypothesis is that projection takes place through perceptual fields, extending out beyond the brain, connecting the seeing animal with that which is seen. Vision is rooted in the activity of the brain, but is not confined to the inside of the head (Sheldrake, 1994; 2003). Like Velmans, I suggest that the formation of these fields depends on the changes occurring in various regions of the brain as vision takes place, influenced by expectations, intentions and memories. Velmans suggests that this projection takes place in a way that is analogous to a field phenomenon, as in a hologram. I suggest that the perceptual projection is not just analogous to but actually is a field phenomenon.

We are used to the idea of fields projecting beyond material bodies, as in the case of magnetic fields around magnets, the earth's gravitational field around the earth, and the electromagnetic fields of mobile phones around the phones themselves. There is nothing unscientific or dualistic about extended fields of influence pervading material bodies and reaching out beyond their surfaces. I suggest

---

[1] For the figure illustrating this, see Velmans' contribution to this volume, p. 111 below.

that minds likewise extend beyond brains through fields. Perceptual fields are related to a broader class of biological fields involved in the organization of developing organisms and in the activity of the nervous system.

The idea of biological fields has been an important aspect of developmental biology since the 1920s, when the hypothesis of morphogenetic fields was first proposed (Gurwitsch, 1922). These fields underlie processes of biological morphogenesis. (Morphogenesis means the coming-into-being of form.) They organize and shape biological development (von Bertalanffy, 1933; Weiss, 1939; Waddington, 1957; Thom, 1975; 1983; Goodwin, 1982; Sheldrake, 1981; 1988). Morphogenetic fields are also active at the molecular level, for example in helping guide the folding of proteins towards their characteristic three-dimensional form, 'choosing' among many possible minimum-energy structures (Sheldrake, 1981).

The concept of morphogenetic fields is widely accepted within developmental biology. The way in which a given cell develops within, say, a developing limb, depends on what Lewis Wolpert has called 'positional information'. This information depends on the cell's position and is specified by a positional or morphogenetic field (Wolpert, 1978; 1980).

Most biologists hope that morphogenetic fields will eventually be explained in terms of the known fields of physics, or in terms of patterns of diffusion of chemicals, or by other known kinds of physico-chemical mechanism (e.g Meinhardt, 1982; Goodwin, 1994). Models of these fields in terms of chemical gradients may indeed help to explain an early stage of morphogenesis, called pattern formation, in which different groups of cells make different proteins (e.g. Wolpert, 1980; Slack and Tannahill, 1992). But morphogenesis itself, the formation of structures like limbs, eyes and flowers, involves more than making the right proteins in the right cells at the right times. The cells, tissues and organs form themselves into specific structures in a way that is still very poorly understood, and it is here that morphogenetic fields would play an essential role shaping and guiding the developmental processes. My proposal is that morphogenetic fields are not just a way of talking about known phenomena like gradients of chemicals, but are a new kind of field (Sheldrake, 1981).

Morphogenetic fields are part of a larger class of fields called morphic fields, which includes behavioural, social and perceptual fields. Such fields can be modelled mathematically in terms of attractors within vector fields (Thom, 1975; 1983; Sheldrake, 1988).

Behavioural fields organize animal behaviour through patterning the otherwise chaotic or indeterminate activity in nervous systems (Sheldrake, 1988; 1999). Social fields coordinate the activity of social groups, including the flight of birds in flocks or swimming of fish in schools, where the whole group can turn rapidly without the individuals bumping into each other (Sheldrake, 2003).

According to this hypothesis, it is in the nature of morphic fields to bind together and coordinate patterns of activity into a larger whole. Morphic fields guide systems under their influence towards attractors, and they stabilize systems through time by means of self-resonance. They are also influenced by a resonance across time and space from previous similar systems, by a process called morphic resonance. Thus they contain an inherent memory, both of system's own past, and a kind of collective or pooled memory from previous similar systems elsewhere. Through repetition a morphic field becomes increasingly habitual. The 'force' these fields exert can be thought of as the force of habit.

The fields themselves are fields of probability, and they influence probabilistic processes; in this sense they resemble the fields of quantum field theory.

The morphic field hypothesis originally grew out of research in developmental and molecular biology. But morphic fields have properties relevant to three aspects of the mind/brain problem. First, by their nature they could connect together patterns of activity in different regions of the brain, and thus help provide a solution to the so-called binding problem. Second, they contain attractors, which organize and give meaning to the entire system, and thus help explain the intentionality of perception; it is *about* something; it is meaningful (Gray, 2004). Third, they link into a single system the subject and the object, the observer and the observed, and extend out beyond the brain to include or enclose the object of perception (Sheldrake, 2003a).

To understand the sense of being stared at, we need a further postulate, namely that these perceptual fields interact with the fields of the person or animal on which attention is focussed. *Ex hypothesi*, all people and animals have their own morphic fields, so this interaction would require an action of like upon like, a field-field interaction (Sheldrake, 2003). Physics already provides many examples of field-field interactions, as in gravitational, electrical, magnetic, electromagnetic and quantum matter fields.

Are perceptual fields real, or are they virtual? They are real in the sense that they are localized in space and time, they resonate with and have effects on the systems under their influence. They impose patterns on the probabilistic activity of nerves and networks of nerves. They interact with other morphic fields, such as those of a person or animal being stared at. But they are virtual in the sense that they are fields of probability or potentiality. They can be modelled mathematically in multidimensional spaces, as in René Thom's models of dynamical attractors within morphogenetic fields. In this sense morphic fields resemble quantum fields, rather than classical electromagnetic or gravitational fields.

This hypothesis might help to explain the sense of being stared at when the looking is direct. But what about the effects of staring through closed circuit television? It is difficult to imagine that perceptual fields first link the observer to the TV screen then extend backwards through the circuitry of the monitor, out through the input wires, out through the camera, and then project through the camera lens to touch the person being observed. The only alternative I can think of is to suppose that seeing the image on the screen somehow sets up a resonant connection with the person whose image is being seen. This could be an instance of morphic resonance, the influence of like upon like across space and time.

The details of how perceptual fields work and how they interact are still unclear. The way in which they can help explain the effects of staring through CCTV is obscure. But even in this vague form, the perceptual field hypothesis has the advantage of making better sense of vision and of the sense of being stared at than the mind-in-the-brain theory and the non-physical projection theory. It also ties in with a wide range of other biological phenomena, including morphogenesis and instinctive behaviour.

V: Interconnections Between the Observer and the Observed in Quantum Physics

There are at least four ways in which quantum physics might be relevant to the sense of being stared at.

The role of the observer

First, the observer and the observed are interconnected: '[Q]uantum physics presents a picture of reality in which observer and observed are inextricably interwoven in an intimate way' (Davies and Gribben, 1991, p. 208). Or as the quantum physicist Bernard D'Espagnat expressed it, 'The doctrine that the world is made up objects whose existence is independent of human consciousness turns out to be in conflict with quantum mechanics and with facts established by experiment' (D'Espagnat, 1979).

The most famous thought experiment on this subject, Schrödinger's cat paradox, implies a spectacular macroscopic effect of observation: staring at a cat can cause it to live or die. A hypothetical cat is confined inside a box containing a glass phial of cyanide; poised above it is a hammer whose fall is triggered when a Geiger counter detects the emission of an alpha particle from a radioactive atom. There is an equal probability that a particle is emitted or not in a given time. The quantum wave of the whole system thus involves a superposition of both possibilities, in one of which the cat is alive and in the other dead. The situation is resolved one way or the other when someone looks into the box and observes the cat, at which stage the wave function 'collapses'.

This thought experiment has generated a long-lasting debate, still unresolved, in theoretical quantum physics. Perhaps the strangest of all interpretations is the many-universe hypothesis. At the moment of observation, the entire universe splits into two coexisting parallel realities, one with a live cat in the box, the other with a dead cat (Davies and Gribben, 1991).

The quantum physicist David Deutsch, a leading proponent of this extravagant hypothesis, postulates that there is 'a huge number of parallel universes, each similar in composition to the tangible one, and each obeying the same laws of physics, but differing in that the particles are in different positions in each universe' (Deutsch, 1997, p. 45).

Compared with an observer splitting the universe by looking at a cat, the sense of being stared at seems conservative.

Photons moving backwards

Second, an interpretation of quantum physics promoted by Richard Feynman emphasizes that there is no difference in nature between a photon moving forwards or backwards in time, from the point of view of electrodynamics. Feynman started from the classical electromagnetic equations of Maxwell, which are symmetrical in relation to time. These equations always give two solutions to describe the propagation of electromagnetic waves, one corresponding to a wave moving forwards in time, and the other to a wave moving backwards in time. Backward moving waves were simply ignored as non-physical until Feynman began to take them seriously.

Waves moving outwards from an electron or radio mast are called 'retarded' waves, because they arrive somewhere else after they have been emitted; waves traveling backwards in time are called 'advanced' waves because they arrive somewhere before they have been emitted.

In what is called the 'Wheeler-Feynman absorber theory', when an electron is agitated, it sends out a retarded wave into the future and an advanced wave into the past. Wherever this wave meets another electron, it excites that electron, which in turn sends out a retarded and advanced wave. The result is an overlapping sea of interacting electromagnetic waves. Thus, 'your eyes *do* emit photons, as part of an exchange with the photons radiated by a source of light ... [T]he old picture of a photon moving from a source of light to our eyes (or to anywhere else) is incomplete; time has no meaning for a photon, and all we can say is that photons have been exchanged between the source of light and our eyes' (Gribben, 1995, pp. 106–7).

John Cramer has developed this approach further in the 'transactional interpretation' of quantum mechanics. He summarizes it as follows: 'The emitter produces a retarded offer wave which travels to the absorber, causing the absorber to produce an advanced confirmation wave which travels back down the track of the offer wave to the emitter ... An observer would perceive only the completed transaction which he could interpret as the passage of a single retarded (i.e. positive energy) photon traveling at the speed of light from emitter to absorber' (Cramer, 1986).

This transactional interpretation of quantum mechanics would be relevant to the sense of being stared at if the advanced wave, emitted from the eye, was coupled to the vision of the perceiver.

Quantum entanglement

The third relevant aspect of quantum mechanics is quantum non-locality or entanglement. It is well established that when pairs of particles, such as photons, are produced from a common source can show correlations in their behaviour over large distances that are inexplicable on the basis of old-style physics. There has been much debate about the significance of this process for macroscopic systems such as ourselves, owing to the 'decoherence' of quantum states in large systems such as brains. Yet some physicists believe that quantum entanglement may be an essential aspect of the way minds work.

Christopher Clarke argues that entanglement may not only play an important part in vision, but also that quantum entanglement is an essential aspect of conscious perception (Clarke, 2004). Consciousness itself somehow arises from entangled systems: 'If the qualitative aspect of perception (the so-called qualia) are produced by quantum entanglement between the states of the brain and the states of perceived objects, then the supports of conscious loci are not just the brain, but the whole of perceived space. In other words "I" am spread out over the universe by virtue of my connectivity with other beings' (Clarke, 2002; p. 177). Clarke further suggests that in living organisms quantum entanglement may helps to account for their holistic properties: 'If we consider a living, and hence coherent, entity, then the entanglement will take over the individual states of the parts, which will no longer be definable, and replace them with the quantum state of the entangled whole' (Clarke, 2002, p. 266).

The psychologist Dean Radin points out that the growing pressure to develop workable quantum computers is rapidly expanding our ability to produce ever more robust forms of entanglement in increasingly complex systems, and predicts that our understanding of what entanglement means will expand rapidly. He paints a future scenario in which researchers will discover that living cells exhibit properties associated with quantum entanglement, giving rise to the idea of bioentanglement, and then to the idea that 'minds and brains are complementary, like particles and waves ... there are interpenetrating mind fields' (Radin, 2004, p.12). He predicts that sooner or later it will be discovered that mind fields are entangled with the rest of the universe. In this scenario, the sense of being stared at would seem relatively straightforward.

Quantum Darwinism

A team of physicists at Los Alamos has recently proposed a form of preferential perception of quantum states that becomes habitual, in a way that sounds not unlike the activity of habitual perceptual fields discussed above (Ollivier et al., 2004).

A *Nature* news report in 2004 explained how this new hypothesis arose from the question, 'If, as quantum mechanics says, observing the world tends to change it, how is it that we can agree on anything at all? Why doesn't each person leave a slightly different version of the world for the next person to find? ' The answer is called quantum Darwinism:

> [C]ertain special states of a system are promoted above others by a quantum form of natural selection.... Information about these states proliferates and gets imprinted on the environment. So observers coming along and looking at the environment in order to get a picture of the world tend to see the same 'preferred' states'.

Rather than decoherence being a problem for this view, it is an essential feature. As Ollivier's co-author Zurek put it, 'Decoherence selects out of the quantum "mush" those states that are stable.' These stable states are called 'pointer' states. Through a 'Darwin-like selection process' these states proliferate as many observers see the same thing. In Zurek's words, 'One might say that pointer states are most 'fit'. They survive monitoring by the environment to leave 'descendents' that inherit their properties' (Ball, 2004).

If a pointer state links an observer to someone she is looking at, such preferred states of quantum decoherence might underlie the sense of being stared at. Indeed a preferred habitual quantum state may be another way of talking about a perceptual field.

VI: Conclusions

Speculations about quantum interconnectedness and about perceptual fields are still vague. But at the same time the conventional idea of a representation or virtual reality display inside the brain is also very vague; it gives no details of the way in which the simulation is produced, the medium in which it occurs, or the means by which is experienced subjectively. Nevertheless, the internal representation theory does make at least one testable prediction: the sense of being stared at should not exist. If vision is confined to the brain, the concentration of attention on a person or an animal should have no effects at a distance, other than those mediated by sound, vision or other recognized senses. The evidence goes against this prediction.

If further research supports the reality of the sense of being stared at, then the existence of this sense will favour theories of vision that involve an interaction between the perceiver and the perceived, and go against theories that confine vision to the inside of the head.

References

Ball, P. (2004), 'Natural selection acts on the quantum world', *news@nature.com* December 23.

Bergson, H. ([1896] English translation 1911), *Matter and Memory* (London: Allen and Unwin).

Clarke, C. (2002), *Living in Connection: Theory and Practice of the New World-View* (Warminster: Creation Spirituality Books).

Clarke, C. (2004), 'Quantum mechanics, consciousness and the self', in *Science, Consciousness and Ultimate Reality*, ed. D. Lorimer (Exeter: Imprint Academic).

Cottrell, J.E. and Winer, G.A. (1974), 'Development on the understanding of perception: The decline of extramission beliefs', *Developmental Psychology*, **30**, pp. 218–28.

Cottrell, J.E., Winer, G.A. & Smith, M.C. (1996), 'Beliefs of children and adults about feeling stares of unseen others', *Developmental Psychology*, **3** (2), pp. 50–61.

Cramer, J. (1986), 'The transactional interpretation of quantum mechanics', *Reviews of Modern Physics*, **58**, pp. 647–88.

Davies, P. and Gribben, J. (1991), *The Matter Myth* (London: Viking).

D'Espagnat, B. (1979), 'The quantum theory and reality', *Scientific American*, November, pp. 158–81.

Dodds, E.R. (1971), 'Supernormal phenomena in classical antiquity', *Proceedings of the Society for Psychical Research*, **55**, pp. 185–237.

Deutsch. D. (1997), *The Fabric of Reality* (London: Allen Lane).

Duncan, T and Kennett, H (2001), *GCSE Physics* (London: Murray).

Dundes, A. ed. (1992), *The Evil Eye: A Casebook* (Madison, WI: University of Wisconsin Press).

Fodor, J.A. and Pylyshyn, Z.W. (1981), 'How direct is visual perception? Some reflections on Gibson's "ecological approach"', *Cognition*, **9**, pp. 139–56.

Gibson, J.J. (1979), *The Ecological Approach to Visual Perception* (Boston, MA: Houghton Mifflin).

Goodwin, B. (1982), 'Development and evolution', *Journal of Theoretical Biology*, **97**, pp. 43–55.

Goodwin, B. (1994), *How the Leopard Changed its Spots* (London: Weidenfeld and Nicholson).

Gray, J. (2004), *Consciousness: Creeping Up on the Hard Problem* (Oxford: Oxford University Press).

Gribben, J. (1995), *Schrödinger's Kittens* (London: Weidenfeld and Nicholson).

Gurwitsch, A. (1922), 'Über den Begriff des embryonales Feldes', *Archiv für Entwicklungs-mechanik*, **51**, pp. 383–415.

James, W. ([1904] 1970), 'Does "consciousness" exist?' Reprinted in *Body and Mind: Readings in Philosophy*, ed. G.N.A. Vesey (London: Allen and Unwin).

Kahn, F. (1949), *The Secret of Life: The Human Machine and How It Works* (London: Odhams).

Lehar, S. (1999), 'Gestalt isomorphism and the quantification of spatial perception', *Gestalt Theory*, **21**, pp. 122–39.

Lehar, S. (2004), 'Gestalt isomorphism and the primacy of subjective conscious experience', *Behavioral and Brain Sciences*, **26**, pp. 375–444.

Lindberg, D.C. (1981), *Theories of Vision from Al-Kindi to Kepler* (Chicago, IL: University of Chicago Press).

Marr, D. (1982), *Vision: A Computational Investigation into the Human Representation and Processing of Visual Information* (New York: W.H. Freeman).

Meinhardt, H. (1982), *Models of Biological Pattern Formation* (London: Academic Press).

Newton, I. (1730), *Opticks*, 4th edition, reprinted 1952 (New York: Dover).

Noë, A. (2002), 'Is the visual world a grand illusion?', *Journal of Consciousness Studies*, **9** (5–6), pp. 1–12.

Ollivier, H., Poulin, D. and Zurek, W. (2004), 'Objective properties from subjective quantum states: Environment as witness', *Physical Review Letters*, **93**, p. 220.

O'Regan, J.K. (1992), 'Solving the "real" mysteries of visual perception: The world as an outside memory', *Canadian Journal of Psychology*, **46**, pp. 461–88.

Piaget, J. (1973), *The Child's Conception of the World* (London: Granada).

Radin, D. (2004), 'Entangled minds', *Shift*, **5**, pp. 10–14.

Russell, B. (1948), *Human Knowledge: Its Scope and Its Limits* (London: Allen and Unwin).

Sheldrake, R. (1981), *A New Science of Life: The Hypothesis of Formative Causation* (London: Blond and Briggs).

Sheldrake, R. (1988), *The Presence of the Past: Morphic Resonance and the Habits of Nature* (London: Collins).

Sheldrake, R. (1994), *Seven Experiments that Could Change the World* (London: Fourth Estate).

Sheldrake, R. (1999), *Dogs that Know When Their Owners Are Coming Home, and Other Unexplained Powers of Animals* (London: Hutchinson).

Sheldrake, R. (2003), *The Sense of Being Stared At, And Other Aspects of the Extended Mind* (London: Hutchinson).

Slack, J.M. and Tannahill, D. (1992), 'Mechanism of anteroposterior axis specification in vertebrates: Lessons from the amphibians',. *Development*, **114**, pp. 285–302.

Takahashi, K. (1992), *The Medieval Latin Traditions of Euclid's Catoptrica* (Kyusu: Kyusu University Press).

Thom, R. (1975), *Structural Stability and Morphogenesis* (Reading, MA: Benjamin).

Thom, R. (1983), *Mathematical Models of Morphogenesis* (Chichester: Horwood).

Thompson, E., Palacios, A. and Varela, F.J. (1992), 'Ways of coloring: Comparative color vision as a case study for cognitive science', *Behavioral and Brain Sciences*, **15**, pp. 1–26.

Velmans, M. (2000), *Understanding Consciousness* (London: Routledge).

Von Bertalanffy, L. (1933), *Modern Theories of Development* (London: Oxford University Press).

Waddington, C.H. (1957), *The Strategy of the Genes* (London: Allen and Unwin).

Weiss, P. (1939), *Principles of Development* (New York: Holt).

Whitehead, A.N. (1925), *Science and the Modern World* (New York: Macmillan).

Winer, G.A. and Cottrell, J.E. (1996a), 'Does anything leave the eye when we see?', *Current Directions in Psychological Science*, **5**, pp. 137–42.

Winer, G.A., Cottrell, J.E., Gregg, V.A., Fournier, J.S., and Bica, L.A. (2002), 'Fundamentally misunderstanding visual perception: Adults' beliefs in visual emissions', *American Psychologist*, **57**, pp. 417–24.

Wolpert, L. (1978), 'Pattern formation in biological development', *Scientific American*, **239** (October), pp. 154–64.

Wolpert, L. (1980), 'Positional information, pattern formation and morphogenesis', in *Morphogenesis and Pattern Formation*, ed. Connelly, T.G., Brinkley, L.L. and Carlson, B.M. (New York: Raven Press).

Zajonc, A. (1993), *Catching the Light: The Entwined History of Light and Mind* (New York: Bantam Books).

Open Peer Commentary

on 'The Sense of Being Stared At' Parts 1 & 2

ANTHONY P. ATKINSON

Staring at the Back of Someone's Head Is No Signal, And a Sense Of Being Stared At Is No Sense

I: Introduction

The first of Sheldrake's twin articles in this edition of the *Journal of Consciousness Studies* presents the case for the existence of a 'sense of being stared at', which is purported to be a capacity to discriminate at above chance levels between being stared at and not being stared at from behind, by an observer who is, on standard accounts of vision, unseen. That case is based on a summary and amalgamation of the results of dozens of experiments, most of them so-called direct-looking experiments (where the observer is present in the room with the subject), along with some experiments that use more indirect methods (where the observer and subject are in separate rooms connected by closed circuit television or one-way mirrors); anecdotal accounts of a sense of being stared at are proffered in a supporting role. In the second of Sheldrake's articles, he presents a case for a radical re-conceptualization of vision, one that, he claims, will allow us to explain how people are apparently sometimes able to tell whether some otherwise unseen person is staring at the back of their heads.[1] In this commentary, I argue that Sheldrake presents and analyses the data in the wrong way, and that labelling such a capacity a sense is a misnomer. I also suggest that there really is no such capacity, but that, to the extent that there is anything substantive and meaningful in the data at all, it indicates a capacity that is rather more cognitive than sensory-perceptual, namely a belief or reasoning bias.

II: Mistaking Signal For Noise

Sheldrake is convinced by the data summarised in his article that at least some people are able, at least some of the time, to tell that someone else is looking at them, even though they are unable to see that person (in the usual sense). Notice that there are two issues here. First, there is the question of whether there is, and ever can be, a signal in the first place; that is, whether the fact that someone is staring at your back can be signalled by that very behaviour alone, without any

---

[1] From what I could fathom from this re-conceptualization of vision, there is also a hint of a putative account not only of the sense of being stared at, but also of why it is only stares that can be discriminated by this 'eyes-in-the-back-of-the-head' capacity. Certainly an account of the former ought to explain the latter issue.

additional behavioural or verbal cues. Second, there is the question of whether people are able to detect such a signal, and if so, how sensitive their ability is to do so. The problem with the first issue is that we have no means by which we can discover the existence of such a signal that is independent of subjective report, of a feeling of being stared at. The prospects of finding such an independent means of measurement are highly remote, despite Sheldrake's brave — but, I have to admit, rather vague and ultimately misguided — attempt to specify, in Part 2 of his piece, a means by which such a signal might manifest itself and a means by which people might be able to detect such a signal. The idea of a 'staring at you' signal, and Sheldrake's specific proposal, are far outside the realms of current scientific knowledge, *pace* Sheldrake's attempt to persuade us otherwise.

The problem I see with respect to the second issue, in addition to what I have already implied, is Sheldrake's presentation of it. I have two points to make, the second relatively minor compared to the first (though nonetheless important). First, consider what Sheldrake says of the participants' task in the typical experimental setup used to test for the presence of a sense of being stared at. In addition to being asked to detect the presence of a stare, Sheldrake claims that: 'The subjects are being asked to detect the *absence* of a stare, an unnatural request with no parallel in real-life conditions' (p. 18). No they are not. The subjects are only being asked to detect the presence of a stare. The task is a simple yes–no task (a well-known variant of the two-alternative forced choice); the participants have to answer either 'yes', the person is staring at me (stare present), or 'no', the person is not staring at me (stare absent). The stare (a signal) is either present or it is not, and in either case there is 'noise', which comprises all other stimuli in the environment transduced by the relevant sense organ (though just what this would amount to in Sheldrake's conception of a sense of being stared at is unclear; see Section III, below), along with the variability in the responses of that sense organ and its associated perceptual mechanisms in the brain. Successful detection of the signal depends on its strength (against the strength of the noise) and the sensitivity of the relevant sensory transducers and relevant neural machinery. Subjects can be either right or wrong about the presence of the signal. They can say the signal is there when it is (a hit or true positive), that it is not there when it is indeed not there (a correct rejection or true negative), that it is there when it is not (a false alarm or false positive), and that it is not there when it is (a miss or false negative). This is the basis of signal detection theory (e.g., Green & Swets, 1966; Stanislaw & Todorov, 1999).

According to signal detection theory, the performance of subjects in yes–no tasks can be fully described by the hit rate (the proportion of hits) and the false alarm rate (the proportion of false alarms). The hit and false alarm rates reflect two factors: the response bias or decision criterion of the participants (how likely they are to respond yes or no to signals of given intensities) and their sensitivity to the signal. Percentage correct scores, which Sheldrake reports and upon which he bases his claims about the existence of a sense of being stared at, reflect sensitivity reliably only in the absence of any response bias. In yes–no tasks, response bias is more likely than in standard two-alternative forced-choice tasks, so reliance on percentage correct scores as measures of sensitivity is problematic. The most widely accepted measure of the sensitivity of subjects is the value of d', which, if certain assumptions are met, is independent of response bias.[2] The formula for calculating d' need not concern us here; it suffices to note that d' expresses a relationship between the hit and false alarm rate, and that a d' value of 0 indicates an inability to distinguish signal from noise, whereas perfect performance is indicated by a d' value of $+\infty$.

Thus the crucial comparisons for the being-stared-at-from-behind experiments discussed by Sheldrake are not the proportion of right versus wrong answers in each of the looking and not looking trials, as he makes out, but rather, the proportion of hits versus false alarms. If we take the values in Sheldrake's Figure 1A (p. 11 above; exact values obtained from Sheldrake, 1999, Table 5), we see that the overall hit rate across these many experiments is 0.59 (i.e., 59%) and the overall false alarm rate is 0.493 (i.e., 49.3%). Plugging these values into the Applet for calculating d' from the hit and false alarm rates provided at http://wise.cgu.edu/sdt/sdt.html yields a d' value of 0.25. On a scale of 0 to $+\infty$, 0.25 is a very small d' value indeed. So how does that compare to typical d' values in other kinds of yes–no perceptual tasks? Azzopardi and Cowey (1997) reported that the sensitivity of a blindsight patient, GY, in detecting the presence of static, vertical, black-and-white, square-wave contrast gratings presented in his blind field ranged from 0.833 for the lowest contrast to 1.354 for the highest contrast. Blake *et al.* (2003) reported that a group of children with autism were impaired relative to a group of typically developing children in being able to discriminate biological motion in point-light displays from phase-scrambled versions of the same displays (i.e., to say whether a person was present in the display or not). The mean d' value for the autistic children was around 1.2, whereas it was around 2.5 for the typically developing children. Grimshaw *et al.* (2004) had participants detect the presence of a target emotion (happy, sad, or angry, depending on the experimental block) amongst a series of facial expressions (happy, sad, angry, or fearful) presented for only 50ms, by requiring them to press a button to indicate 'yes' (target present) or 'no' (target absent). The mean d' values were 2.5 for sad, 2.6 for angry, and 3.45 for happy targets. In sum, if there really is a 'staring at you' signal, then a d' value of around 0.25 indicates that we are not very sensitive to that signal at all.

Furthermore, consider that a d' value as low as 0.25 indicates that subjects with a liberal response criterion (i.e., with a response bias towards saying 'yes') produced a high proportion of hits but also an almost equally high proportion of false alarms, whereas subjects with a conservative response criterion (i.e., a response bias towards saying 'no') produced a low proportion of hits and a low

---

[2] This is not the place to discuss what those assumptions are. For the sake of argument, I am assuming that these assumptions are upheld in the present case. There are other, non-parametric measures of sensitivity, which can be used if these assumptions relating to the use of d', and thus to the independence of this measure of sensitivity from response bias, do not hold. See Stanislaw & Todorov (1999) for discussion.

(again, nearing equal) proportion of false alarms. With rather higher d' values, as the response criterion decreases (i.e., gets more liberal), the false alarm rate does not increase as rapidly as the hit rate. (A nice graphical illustration of this is provided at http://wise.cgu.edu/sdt/sdt.html.) Presenting the data as Sheldrake does (i.e., as mean percentages correct and incorrect in the looking and not looking trials) obscures possibly important individual differences between subjects in their response criteria. Indeed, if, as I will suggest in Section IV, the findings in the being-stared-at-from-behind experiments reflect a belief or reasoning bias operating in some (but not all) subjects, rather than a sensory-perceptual capacity to detect whether someone is staring at the back of one's head or not, then high proportions of both hits and false alarms is exactly what we would expect to find.

The second point I wish to raise regarding Sheldrake's presentation of the apparent ability of people to detect when they are being stared at from behind is this. Sheldrake emphasises the 'astronomically significant' (p. 14) statistical results obtained when the results of many direct looking experiments are combined, resulting in analyses over 'tens of thousands of trials' (p. 14). If we set aside worries about conducting statistical tests on the combined results of studies that likely differed, even subtly, in various ways (more on which below), such significance values are indeed very impressive. Lest we forget, however, significance values tell us only about the *reliability* of any effect (the probability that the results are due to chance, rather than to the effect or variable in question), not about the *strength* or size of such an effect. Now Sheldrake does not conflate these two issues. Nonetheless, it is important that the distinction is emphasised, for a statistically naïve reader might take Sheldrake's point to imply that consistent findings of around 55% correct guesses in direct looking experiments (5% above chance) is a large effect, when it is in fact very small. Just how small the reported effects are, we do not know. For measures of effect size are reasonably straightforward to calculate, and are included as output options in most statistics computer packages, yet Sheldrake does not report the effect sizes of any of the experiments he reports (admittedly, nor do the majority of published studies in psychology).

In the previous paragraph I mentioned that there are legitimate concerns about conducting statistical tests on the combined results of different studies, even if those studies have essentially identical experimental setups. One concern is that the subjects' expectations or motivation may vary across studies, depending on varying demand characteristics, as the result of even small differences in experimental procedures, and experimenter expectancy effects. This is a particular problem in the case of forced-choice yes–no tasks, for as signal detection theory teaches us, a subject's response criterion, and thus the proportions of hits and false alarms, can vary even when the signal intensity and the subject's sensitivity to that signal remain constant. Clear demonstrations of such changes in subjects' response criteria are provided by studies in which the payoffs for the four possible responses are manipulated (e.g., varying the size of rewards for hits and correct rejections, and the size of penalties for false alarms and misses).

Nevertheless, subjects' response criteria can also vary as a function of more subtle factors, such as differences in demand characteristics and experimenter expectancy effects.

III: In What Sense Is the Sense of Being Stared At a Sense?

If there is a *sense* of being stared at, then it is rather different from any of our other senses. Each of our six main senses (vision, hearing, smell, touch, taste, proprioception) conveys a multitude of messages; indeed, in some cases, the number and variety of the informational contents are essentially boundless. The more complex the sensory organs and the neural systems devoted to processing information transduced by those organs, the more and richer the messages that are conveyed. A sense of being stared at, in contrast, is held to convey only one possible message: 'someone is staring at me'. That would be a very primitive sense indeed. Granted, there are organisms out there that have primitive sense organs of sorts, sense organs that convey only one message. Certain single-cell organisms, some jellyfish, starfish and leeches, for example, can sense the presence of light somewhere nearby (thanks to their light-sensitive body surfaces, rather than to their possession of eyes, as such), but cannot distinguish amongst different sources of light or even what direction it is coming from, and certainly cannot use that light to form an image of any sort (example borrowed from Dawkins, 1996). Is Sheldrake proposing that we have some equally primitive sense organ and thus sensory capacity? I doubt it. As becomes clear in the second of Sheldrake's articles, he wants to include the sense of being stared at not as a separate sense, in the way vision or hearing are senses (or even in the way that a primitive capacity to detect the presence of light might be regarded as a sense), but as an aspect of vision — albeit only after a radical re-conceptualisation of that sense.

IV: The Sense of Being Stared At Is Likely to be a Belief or Reasoning Bias

A telling allusion to what I think is really going on in the being-stared-at-from-behind experiments is made by Sheldrake on p. 25, where he mentions Jonathan Jones's unpublished finding of higher levels of arousal in people with high scores on the Schizotypal Personality Questionnaire when they were being stared at from behind, compared to when they were not being stared at, whereas low scorers did not differ in their arousal levels. This is indeed an interesting finding, and, I have to concede, might be considered to count against the sceptical position I am advancing. That said, to my knowledge this finding has not been replicated in a peer-reviewed published study, and so must be taken with a pinch of salt. However, the main point I wish to draw from this paragraph of Sheldrake's article is not related to this particular finding, but rather, to the suggestion that people who tend towards a schizotypal personality type differ from people who are less schizotypic in respect of their responses in the being-stared-at-from-behind experiments. Rather than being more *sensitive* to having the back of their heads stared at, I suggest that people with schizotypal tendencies manifest an amplified *response* or *reasoning bias*.

Reasoning biases are common in schizophrenia, especially in people with persecutory delusions. Schizophrenics with persecutory delusions are more likely to jump to conclusions on the basis of insufficient information than non-deluded controls (e.g. Huq *et al.*, 1988; Dudley *et al.*, 1997a,b), and have a greater tendency to attribute negative events to external personal causes (e.g. Kaney & Bentall, 1989; Lyon *et al.*, 1994). People with persecutory delusions also tend to have biased attention and memory for material associated with personal threat, and appear to experience a heightened state of vigilance for threat in inappropriate or ambiguous contexts, believing there to be threat without supporting evidence (e.g. Bentall *et al.*, 1995; Kaney *et al.*, 1992; 1997). (For reviews, see Blackwood *et al.*, 2001; Garety & Freeman, 1999.) All this is consistent with the possibility that schizophrenics with persecutory delusions will tend to show a bias towards answering 'yes' in the being-stared-at-from-behind experiments discussed by Sheldrake. To the extent that persecutory delusions and other schizotypy tendencies in the normal population are like attenuated forms of those symptoms in clinically psychotic individuals, we might also expect that a response bias for answering 'yes' in being-stared-at-from-behind experiments will positively correlate with the degree of delusional ideation and schizotypy personality style in non-clinical groups. Interestingly, Brébion *et al.* (2000) found that schizophrenics with higher hallucination scores had a tendency to respond with a high rate of false alarms in a recognition memory test for items presented either verbally or visually, and that both hallucinators and delusional patients were more likely to mistake imagined (verbally presented) items as pictures they had actually perceived, suggesting that such people may show similar response biases in the being-stared-at-from-behind experiments. I recommend that these predictions be tested in future research on the (misnamed) sense of being stared at.

References

Azzopardi, P. & Cowey, A. (1997), 'Is blindsight like normal, near-threshold vision?' *Proceedings of the National Academy of Sciences*, **94**, pp. 14190–4.

Bentall, R.P., Kaney, S. & Bowen-Jones, K. (1995), 'Persecutory delusions and recall of threat-related, depression-related, and neutral words', *Cognitive Therapy and Research*, **19**, pp. 445–57.

Blackwood, N.J., Howard, R.J., Bentall, R.P. & Murray, R.M. (2001), 'Cognitive neuropsychiatric models of persecutory delusions', *American Journal of Psychiatry*, **158**, pp. 527–39.

Blake, R., Turner, L.M., Smoski, M.J., Pozdol, S.L. & Stone, W.L. (2003), 'Visual recognition of biological motion is impaired in children with autism', *Psychological Science*, **14**, pp. 151–7.

Brébion, G., Amador, X., David, A., Malaspina, D., Sharif, Z. & Gorman, J.M. (2000), 'Positive symptomatology and source-monitoring failure in schizophrenia: An analysis of symptom-specific effects', *Psychiatry Research*, **95**, pp. 119–31.

Dawkins, R. (1996), *Climbing Mount Improbable* (London: Viking/ Penguin).

Dudley, R.E., John, C.H., Young, A.W. & Over, D.E. (1997a), 'The effect of self-referent material on the reasoning of people with delusions', *British Journal of Clinical Psychology*, **36**, pp. 575–84.

Dudley, R.E., John, C.H., Young, A.W. & Over, D.E. (1997b), 'Normal and abnormal reasoning in people with delusions', *British Journal of Clinical Psychology*, **36**, pp. 243–58.

Garety, P.A. & Freeman, D. (1999), 'Cognitive approaches to delusions: A critical review of theories and evidence', *British Journal of Clinical Psychology*, **38**, pp. 113–54.

Green, D.M. & Swets, J.A. (1966), *Signal Detection Theory and Psychophysics* (New York: Wiley).

Grimshaw, G.M., Bulman-Fleming, M.B. & Ngo, C. (2004), 'A signal-detection analysis of sex differences in the perception of emotional faces', *Brain and Cognition*, **54**, pp. 248–50.

Huq, S.F., Garety, P.A., & Hemsley, D.R. (1988), 'Probabilistic judgements in deluded and non-deluded subjects', *Quarterly Journal of Experimental Psychology, A*, **40**, pp. 801–12.

Kaney, S. & Bentall, R.P. (1989), 'Persecutory delusions and attributional style', *British Journal of Medical Psychology*, **62**, pp. 191–8.

Kaney, S., Bowen-Jones, K., Dewey, M.E. & Bentall, R.P. (1997), 'Two predictions about paranoid ideation: Deluded, depressed and normal participants' subjective frequency and consensus judgments for positive, neutral and negative events', *British Journal of Clinical Psychology*, **36**, pp. 349–64.

Kaney, S., Wolfenden, M., Dewey, M.E. & Bentall, R. P. (1992), 'Persecutory delusions and recall of threatening propositions', *British Journal of Clinical Psychology*, **31**, pp. 85–7.

Lyon, H.M., Kaney, S. & Bentall, R.P. (1994), 'The defensive function of persecutory delusions: Evidence from attribution tasks', *British Journal of Psychiatry*, **164**, pp. 637–46.

Sheldrake, R. (1999), 'The "sense of being stared at" confirmed by simple experiments', *Biology Forum*, **92**, pp. 53–76.

Stanislaw, H., & Todorov, N. (1999), 'Calculation of signal detection theory measures', *Behavior Research Methods, Instruments, and Computers*, **31**, pp. 137–49.

IAN S. BAKER[3]

Nomenclature and Methodology

In his first paper Sheldrake attempts to uncover whether or not the 'sense of being stared at' is real or illusory, concluding that 'the great majority of the evidence supports the reality of this sense' (p. 29). I would like to discuss some of the issues that he raises and how they pertain to his central argument and the body of evidence for and against remote staring detection. I will be focussing most of my comments on part one of his paper.

I have divided my comments into three main areas. First, I will discuss the nomenclature that Sheldrake uses in the paper and which is used in the field as a whole to describe this phenomenon and why a consensus is required. Secondly, I will illustrate how there are issues between the different methodologies used in this area concerning two subtly different senses of the concept of ecological validity, namely: realism and generalisability. Finally, I will show how the CCTV-based method offers a superior methodology for the investigation of remote staring detection, and that it represents a considerably different methodology to the other methods listed. This difference, both in terms of the greater robustness and validity when compared to the other approaches, means that the results from the CCTV method have to be considered separately to the other results. This has consequences for the main thrust of the argument that Sheldrake puts forward in this paper.

---

[3] I would like to thank Paul Stevens and Claudia Coelho for their helpful comments on an earlier version of this commentary.

I: Definition

As Sheldrake notes, the 'sense of being stared at' has been investigated for over 100 years, with the majority of the research being conducted from the early 1990s onwards. I would initially like to raise an important point about the terminology in use in this area. Sheldrake uses the term 'the sense of being stared at' to define what Braud *et al.* (1993a,b) describe anecdotally as '[having the] feeling that someone was staring at you from behind and, upon turning around, [finding out that] you were correct' (1993a, p. 373) and operationally as 'the purported ability to detect when one is being watched or stared at by someone situated beyond the range of the conventional senses' (1993b: p. 391).

However, the term that Sheldrake uses is potentially misleading, as it does not define whether or not the stare is conventional in origin, or beyond the range of the conventional senses. An individual could be uncomfortable due to the sensation provided from someone staring at them directly from the front. I advocate the term '*remote staring detection*', not only because remote staring has been used more often in the research than any other term, but also because it defines the three core elements of this phenomenon; first, due to the way that the experiments are designed they are testing if the individual is *detecting* the stare of another. Secondly, the term '*remote*' makes the clear distinction that we are talking about a stare beyond the range of the conventional senses. Finally, the individual is generally '*staring*', a term that is sometimes removed in other nomenclature defining this phenomenon (e.g., 'unseen gaze', 'covert observation', etc.), although it is of particular importance when defining the nature of the phenomenon. There has been a debate in the social psychology literature on interpersonal interaction about the use of particular terms to describe certain visual interactions, with research demonstrating that the term 'staring' is consistently placed at the most extreme end of a scale in terms of the length of time of an eye-fixation (Kirkland and Lewis, 1976; Baker, 2001). Ellsworth *et al.* (1972), made an important definition of staring for their study examining the social impact of staring when they defined it as 'a gaze or look that persists regardless of the behaviour of the other person' (p. 303). Most eye-based dyadic interactions employ a complex relationship of 'mutual gaze' (Argyle and Cook, 1976; Argyle, 1988) between the two individuals, which provides several different types of communication (Kleinke, 1986). However, staring represents an anomaly to this because it remains fixed regardless of the other person's behaviour. Therefore 'staring' is an important term with which to frame remote staring detection, as the stare from the remote individual continues regardless of the behaviour of the individual being stared at. Although there might be some form of interaction between the two individuals, from a purely descriptive position, the term 'remote staring detection' appears to be more appropriate than any other term used to describe this particular phenomenon.

II: Issues of Ecological Validity

One of the main issues surrounding the research into remote staring detection is ecological validity. This issue is complex, and weaves its way throughout many of the different areas of the literature. For example, is the use of direct looking methods more ecologically valid than the separation of the individuals involved by a CCTV link? Is the use of conscious guessing more ecologically valid than the use of unconscious physiological measures? These questions have implications for the controls used in these experiments and how they might restrict the investigation of the real life phenomenon.

Part of the problem is that one can identify two subtly different meanings of the concept of ecological validity that need to be teased apart in any discussion of the validity of different methods used to investigate remote staring detection. First, there is the issue of *generalisability* — can the data obtained from a particular method be generalised to the real life phenomenon that the experiment is attempting to measure? In relation to this issue the discussion will focus specifically on the extent to which the laboratory-based measurements of electrodermal activity can be assumed to be present in all instances of remote staring detection. Secondly, there is the issue of *realism*, which refers to how closely a particular method recreates the phenomenon as one assumes it happens in 'real life'. In relation to this issue, the discussion will focus on whether or not the direct looking experiments are a closer representation of the real-life phenomenon of remote staring detection than the CCTV laboratory-based experiments. I will now examine both of these issues in detail.

Realism

Throughout his paper, Sheldrake refers to different types of research as evidence for or against remote staring detection, highlighting two particular methodologies: the 'direct looking' and the 'CCTV-based' experiments. These different types of methodology can be broadly placed along the continuum that I have outlined in Figure 1. I have also included two additional approaches that he does not clearly place into this classification; namely his own 'Window' experiments, where the starer and staree[4] are separated by a window (Sheldrake, 2000), and the 'One-way Mirror' experiments, where the starer and staree are separated by a one-way mirror.[5]

Figure 1 demonstrates the methodological development and increasing sophistication of the remote staring detection studies. This development has been gradual over the past 100 years, although some researchers, Sheldrake included, have advocated a return to simpler measures. For example, Sheldrake has argued that

---

[4] The 'staree' is the individual who is being stared at. The 'starer' is the individual who is doing the staring.

[5] The terms 'one-way' and 'two-way' mirror are interchangeable and refer to a sheet of metal-coated glass which reflects approximately half of the light and allows the rest to pass through it. When placed in a wall between rooms where one room is dark and the other is well lit, it is possible to see clearly through the mirror into the lighter room from the darker one, but it appears to be a normal mirror from the lighter room.

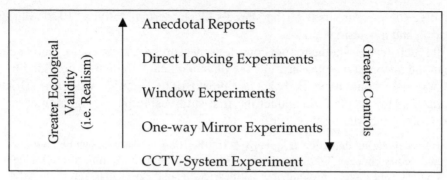

Figure 1. Continuum of remote staring detection studies

'direct-looking tests are far easier to perform than CCTV trials' (p. 14) and that, 'a great advantage of simple experiments in which subjects make conscious guesses is that they enable many more people to take part in this research than the CCTV method. They are also closer to the real life phenomenon' (Sheldrake, 2001, p. 122). He has argued this because typically, with many experiments, as the degree of control over extraneous variables decreases, the degree of the realism element of ecological validity increases (as noted in Figure 1). However, this might not necessarily be the case in the remote staring detection literature.

There has been a dramatic rise in CCTV-systems for everyday surveillance by businesses, and local and national government, particularly in the UK, over the past 10 years. This means that people are observed via CCTV on a daily basis, (as Sheldrake himself notes, p. 22). In fact, it has been estimated, based on surveys on the proliferation of CCTV systems in London, that as of 2003 there were as many as 4.2 million CCTV cameras in the UK, which translates as one camera for every 14 people (McCahill and Norris, 2003, as cited by Norris, McCahill and Wood, 2004). The experiments that used CCTV methodologies recreate this, and therefore are equally ecologically valid to the other methodologies. They are recreating an everyday experience from real life, although it might be different from the type of experience recreated by the direct looking experiments. As Sheldrake notes in his paper (p. 22), and in his previous work (Sheldrake, 2003), his interviews of personnel in the surveillance industry suggest that people do detect being watched via CCTV in real life.

Generalisability

An aspect of methodology where Sheldrake does not draw enough of a distinction in his paper is the difference between conscious and unconscious remote staring detection. Within the literature, conscious measures commonly involve the staree verbally indicating or writing down whether or not they think they are being stared at during a particular epoch.[6] In contrast, the unconscious measures

[6] This refers to a period of time in which a particular stimulus is administered; in this case a remote stare or a rest period (i.e., no stare). Typically these periods last between five to 30 seconds in these experiments.

involve the measurement of the staree's electrodermal activity (EDA) during staring and no-staring epochs.

It is debateable whether or not conscious measures are more ecologically valid than the unconscious measures, as the physiological stimulation provided by a remote stare would most likely act as a precursor to cognitive awareness. Braud *et al.* (1993a) decided to conduct the first study using physiological measures because of this, stating that,

> [remote] staring detection frequently takes the form of spontaneous behavioural and bodily changes. Often, such changes are reported to be rich in physiological content (for example, tingling of the skin, prickling of the neck hairs) and automatic movements (for example, spontaneous head turning, unplanned glances). Higher cognitive functions seem to play minor roles in these staring detection contexts. (Braud *et al.*, 1993a, p. 376–7)

In fact, they also suggest, when discussing previous research using direct looking methodologies employing conscious guessing, that 'such a procedure would be expected to maximise possible cognitive interferences and distortions of subtle internal staring-related cues' (Braud *et al.*, 1993a, p. 376). Therefore, measuring physiological arousal could be more ecologically valid than the behavioural measures, as the information from processing the unconscious, physiological stimulus of the remote stare is not reaching conscious awareness. By measuring the 'pure' unconscious physiological reaction we are avoiding the 'contaminated' cognitive measure. This type of processing of stimuli without conscious awareness has been noted in other areas, such as: change blindness (see O'Regan, 2003, for review) and perception without awareness (see Pessoa, 2005, for review).

III: Can the EDA-CCTV and Direct Looking Methods Be Directly Compared?

The use of EDA measures, with the controls that are implicit in their use, are normally combined with the CCTV method, mainly because of the controls both methods provide, and because they require considerable resources that combine well in the laboratory. These experiments involve separating the starer and staree into different rooms and measuring the EDA of the staree during randomly-scheduled epochs when the starer stares or does not stare at them via the CCTV system. This combination of EDA and CCTV (or EDA-CCTV) provides an even more robust methodology, and *all* of the 15 experiments (from nine studies) that Schmidt *et al.* (2004) included in their meta-analysis of EDA-based remote staring detection studies combined the CCTV method with the physiological measure. Schmidt *et al.* (2004) scrutinised the studies for a variety of issues concerning the veracity of the method, such as: safeguards, the quality of the specific methodology for electrodermal measurement, and overall methodological quality. They found a significant, but small, effect (Cohen's $d = .13$, $p = .01$) across all of the studies.

The size of this effect is also an important factor when comparing the CCTV method with the other methods, particularly the 'direct looking' experiments. Sheldrake claims in his paper that the direct looking experiments have an overall significance[7] value of $p < 1 \times 10^{-20}$ (p. 15). However, as was pointed out above, Schmidt *et al.*'s (2004) meta-analysis found that the EDA-CCTV remote staring detection studies had a far smaller overall significance value of $p = .01$. These significance levels clearly do not match, and the difference between them is readily apparent: *the larger the significance value, the less robust the controls.* Even if a less conservative estimate is used, by examining the meta-analysis of the EDA-based remote staring detection studies by Schlitz and Braud (1997), there is still an enormous discrepancy between the significance of the effect that Sheldrake notes and the significance size that Schlitz and Braud (1997) notes ($r = .25, p = .00005$). There is obviously a significant effect in the remote staring detection studies, as the well-controlled EDA-CCTV studies demonstrate, but there is a strong suggestion that at least part of the disproportionately high significance level of the direct looking experiments could be due to a lack of adequate controls.

The CCTV method has become increasingly divorced from the others in the continuum. Researchers employing the other methodologies in the continuum have gone to great efforts in their attempts to reduce extraneous variables and sources of sensory leakage, but CCTV is the only method that can categorically claim to have achieved this. It does not fall foul of the possible artefacts that Sheldrake describes (p. 21), and he in fact relies upon the results from studies that employed the CCTV method in order to bolster his argument. As soon as these methods are separated and the CCTV method is no longer used to provide support, Sheldrake's arguments against possible artefacts explaining the remote staring effect are forced to rely solely upon less secure methods and unverifiable anecdotal reports. For example, when he argues against 'subtle sensory cues', he states that, 'in addition, positive results in experiments using one-way mirrors and CCTV seem to eliminate the possibility of sensory cues.' When arguing against cheating, he again appeals to methods 'separating lookers and subjects by ... one-way mirrors or by closed circuit television' (p. 21) providing positive results to show that this remains an impossible criticism for all of the studies, without any regard for the methodology used. Finally, when arguing against hand scoring errors, he again relies on the CCTV method to bolster his argument as he states 'also, there was no hand scoring in the CCTV trials' (p. 21).

The use of the combined method of CCTV and electrodermal activity measurement demonstrates such a high degree of methodological and conceptual difference when compared to other studies in the continuum, that they might represent remote staring detection under the best controlled circumstances, or they might represent a subtly different phenomenon altogether. The effect sizes noted under these conditions are similar to the effect sizes noted under other

---

[7] It would have been very useful if Sheldrake had provided an overall effect size in addition to this significance level, and to have had a detailed rationale and description of the process of calculation that led him to conclude this overall level of significance for the direct looking experiments.

DMILS (Direct Mental Interaction between Living Systems) studies that have employed electrodermal activity as a dependent measure (i.e. $d = .11, p = .001$, as reported by Schmidt *et al.*, 2004). It is possible that this represents a similarity between EDA-CCTV and the wider DMILS effects, which might be a related process, but not necessarily the same as the potential remote staring detection effect observed in the direct looking experiments. In the second part of Sheldrake's paper, he discusses remote staring detection and he speculates how it might be related to extramission theory[8] and 'perceptual fields'. However, Sheldrake cannot easily incorporate the findings from the CCTV method, stating, 'the way in which they can help explain the effects of staring through CCTV is obscure' (p. 44), demonstrating that, from his theoretical standpoint, the CCTV method is incomparable with the other methods. We do not yet fully understand the significant effect obtained using the CCTV method, and how these findings are related to the data from the other remote staring detection experiments. We need to clarify the issue with further experimentation examining more detailed physiological reactions to a remote starer separated via a CCTV link, and analysis comparing the validity of the different methods.

IV: Conclusions

There are two main inconsistencies in Sheldrake's argument. First, he relies upon the EDA-CCTV studies to strengthen his argument that the evidence obtained from the direct-looking experiments demonstrate that remote staring detection is a real phenomenon. However, there are considerable methodological differences between these two methods that make a direct comparison difficult. The EDA-CCTV studies are well-controlled laboratory experiments that carefully separate the starer and staree and rely upon unconscious measures. In contrast, the direct-looking experiments cannot incorporate as robust controls due to their very design and their reliance upon conscious guessing. Moreover, the EDA-CCTV studies have demonstrated a significant, if small, effect of remote staring detection on their own, and it is unnecessary to incorporate them with the other, less-controlled studies. It is, however, necessary for the two approaches to stand and be evaluated on their own robustness and validity. The combined EDA-CCTV approach has largely stood up to independent, rigorous statistical and methodological scrutiny, thanks mainly to Schmidt *et al.*'s (2004) meta-analysis; the remote staring detection studies that employed conscious guessing and direct looking have yet to do so.

Secondly, Sheldrake admits in the second part of his paper that the results from the EDA-CCTV studies do not easily fit into the perceptual fields theory that his is advocating to explain remote staring detection. Essentially, in his paper Sheldrake is attempting to have the best of both worlds; he is happy to use the more robust empirical evidence from the EDA-CCTV studies to back up his claims from the direct-looking experiments, but then sidelines the EDA-CCTV

---

[8] Extramission theory is described as the concept that 'vision involve[s] emissions from the eye' (Cottrell *et al.*, 1996: p. 50).

studies from his perceptual fields theory because there is difficulty in incorporating them conceptually.

In conclusion, I would agree with Sheldrake that there is promising evidence that remote staring detection is a real phenomenon, although there is much research required to reveal its nature. However, the evidence comes almost entirely from the well-controlled EDA-CCTV lab-based studies that need to be considered separately from the other approaches.

References

Argyle, M. (1988), *Bodily Communication* (London: Routledge).

Argyle, M. & Cook, M. (1976), *Gaze and Mutual Gaze* (Cambridge University Press).

Baker, I.S. (2001), *The relationship of gaze-avoidance to shyness and belief in the power of gaze, and an analysis of vocabulary for eye-fixation research.* Unpublished Master's thesis, University of Edinburgh, Edinburgh, Scotland, UK.

Braud, W., Shafer, D. & Andrews, S. (1993a), 'Reactions to an unseen gaze (remote attention): A review, with new data on autonomic staring detection', *Journal of Parapsychology*, **57**, pp. 373–90.

Braud, W., Shafer, D. & Andrews, S. (1993b), 'Further studies of autonomic detection of remote staring: Replications, new control procedures, and personality correlates', *Journal of Parapsychology*, **57**, pp. 391–409.

Cottrell, J.E., Winer, G.A. & Smith, M.C. (1996), 'Beliefs of children and adults about feeling stares of unseen others', *Developmental Psychology*, **32** (1), pp. 50–61.

Ellsworth, P.C., Carlsmith, J.M. & Henson, A. (1972), 'The stare as a stimulus to flight in human subjects: A series of field experiments', *Journal of Personality and Social Psychology*, **21**, pp. 302–11.

Kirkland, J. & Lewis, C. (1976), 'Glance, look, gaze, and stare: A vocabulary for eye-fixation research', *Perceptual and Motor Skills*, **43** (3), p. 1278.

Kleinke, C.L. (1986), 'Gaze and eye contact: A research review', *Psychological Bulletin*, **100** (1), pp. 78–100.

Norris, C., McCahill, M. and Wood, D. (2004), 'The growth of CCTV: A global perspective on the international diffusion of video surveillance in publicly accessible space', *Surveillance and Society*, **2** (2/3), pp. 110–35.

O'Regan, J.K. (2003), 'Change blindness', in *Encyclopaedia of Cognitive Science*, ed. L. Nadel (London: Nature Publishing Group).

Pessoa, L. (2005), 'To what extent are emotional visual stimuli processed without attention and awareness?', *Current Opinion in Neurobiology*, **15**, pp. 188–96.

Schlitz, M. & Braud, W. (1997), 'Distant intentionality and healing: Assessing the evidence', *Alternative Therapies*, **3** (6), pp. 62–73.

Schmidt, S., Schneider, R., Utts, J. & Walach, H. (2004), 'Distant intentionality and the feeling of being stared at: Two meta-analyses', *British Journal of Psychology*, **95**, pp. 235–47.

Sheldrake, R. (2000), 'The "sense of being stared at" does not depend on known sensory cues', *Biology Forum*, **93**, pp. 209–24.

Sheldrake, R. (2001), 'Experiments on the sense of being stared at: The elimination of possible artefacts', *Journal of the Society for Psychical Research*, **65**, pp. 122–37.

Sheldrake, R. (2003), *The Sense of Being Stared At, And Other Aspects of the Extended Mind* (London: Hutchinson).

SUSAN BLACKMORE

Confusion Worse Confounded

Sheldrake's two papers are so deeply confused that they should never have been published in JCS. Given that they are published I shall discuss just two worrying confusions; one from each paper.

In Part 1, Sheldrake consistently mixes up the sense of being stared at that derives from the normal senses of vision or hearing, with a putative sense that he claims can operate without normal sensory cues. He might have avoided confusion by giving a name to this proposed paranormal sense, and then made clear, throughout the paper, which he was referring to at different times, but he did not. The reader might try to understand the paper by assuming that when Sheldrake talks about 'the sense of being stared at' he always means this proposed paranormal sense, but this is not so; he uses the same phrase to refer to the normal sense. For example, in the opening quotation from Conan Doyle the man looks up to meet the eyes of the person staring at him, implying that the starer was probably visible in peripheral vision.

This confusion permeates the paper. Detectives should not stare at someone's back for the obvious reason that they might not be able to avert their gaze fast enough, or convincingly enough, if the person happens to turn round. Detection with binoculars might seem impossible by normal means, but binocular lenses can have highly reflective surfaces and may look like eyes from a distance. The surveys discussed seem to include some questions that refer only to a paranormal sense and some that might include normal sensing. This means that when Sheldrake discusses the evolutionary function of the sense of being stared at the reader cannot tell whether he means a normal or paranormal sense. Obviously there would be an evolutionary advantage in being able to detect another's gaze and in fact we, and other species, have visual systems designed to be good at this. A pair of eyes is a salient stimulus. We can pick it out easily from complex scenes, attention is automatically drawn to it, and eye movements are made towards it without prior identification. We can also tell from very small differences whether someone is looking straight at us and focussing on us, or not.

Sheldrake asserts that research has neglected the sense of being stared at because people believe it is impossible. Unless he makes it clear that he is referring to a paranormal sense, this claim is ridiculous. He also refers to a taboo against psychic phenomena. As a former parapsychologist, I do not believe there is any such taboo. The fact is that evidence for paranormal phenomena is weak and usually unreplicable, and there is no plausible theory to explain such evidence as there is. Most scientists choose not to investigate paranormal claims, not because of a taboo, but because they have more promising and exciting things to spend their precious time and research resources on.

There follows a review of experiments some of which were done under conditions that would rule out the use of the normal senses, and some of which would not. Sheldrake admits to the flaws in some of these experiments but then goes on to use all of them — flawed or not — for his assessment of the overall pattern of results. He also gives detailed results of some highly flawed studies but then gives only a cursory description of experiments that would, if valid, be very impressive.

Finally, Sheldrake's conclusion reveals the same confusion. Of course most people say they have sensed when they are being stared at. It is a normal, evolved, human talent. Whether there is also a paranormal ability to detect staring, as Sheldrake seems to believe, remains unknown, but we will not get closer to knowing the truth by reading this misleading and confused paper.

In Part 2 the entire discussion is marred by a confusion between 'active v. passive theories' and 'intromission v extramission theories'. Sheldrake points out that intromission theories have tended to regard vision as passive while extramission theories have tended to regard it as active. This may be true as a historical fact but this is no reason to conflate two fundamentally different distinctions. All modern theories of vision are intromission theories; they assume that light enters the eye and that nothing leaves it. This fits with the physics of light, the structure of the eye, and the principles of sensory systems. Any theory that proposes, as Sheldrake does, that 'An influence seems to pass from the observer to the observed' (p. 32) is a paranormal theory. The problem for normal theories of vision is to understand how incoming information eventually leads to visually guided behaviour and visual experience, and they vary from more active to more passive theories. There has recently been a revival of Gibson's ecological approach to vision and renewed enthusiasm for so-called active and embodied theories of vision, but these do not involve anything leaving the eye and projecting out into the world; their main point is to emphasise how much active processing of the incoming information has to be achieved.

The most extreme of these theories is probably O'Regan and Noë's (2001) sensorimotor theory of vision. This does away entirely with any notion of a picture-like representation in the visual system and replaces it with the idea that vision is a kind of action; seeing is doing. As they put it, seeing is mastering sensorimotor contingencies, or playing with the relationships between one's own actions and the changing input. This is an active theory par excellence but it contains no hint of extramission. Sheldrake praises Gibson's theory because it 'leaves open the possibility of an interaction between the perceiver and the perceived' (p. 41). But this is crazy — for what theory does not? Vision is and must be an ongoing interaction between the perceiver and perceived. By confusing two fundamentally different distinctions between theories of vision Sheldrake has created nothing but an unhelpful muddle.

Reference

O'Regan, J.K. and Noë, A. (2001), 'A sensorimotor account of vision and visual consciousness', *Behavioral and Brain Sciences*, **24** (5), pp. 939–1011.

WILLIAM BRAUD

The Sense of Being Stared At:
Fictional, Physical, Perceptual, or Attentional/Intentional?

According to a well-known adage of folk psychology, 'where there is smoke, there is fire'. In his two-part contribution to this symposium on 'the sense of being stared at', Rupert Sheldrake examines some of the *smoke* (fictional allusions, anecdotal observations and reports, and the persisting lore) surrounding this alleged phenomenon and attempts to determine whether such smoke might indeed be accompanied by some actual *fire* (valid and reliable evidence for the existence of the staring phenomenon). In this effort, he provides an extensive and inclusive account of his own research findings and those of other investigators.

Many contemporary professional psychologists and consciousness researchers would qualify the smoke/fire metaphor. They could suggest that smoke might indicate where a fire may once have been rather than where one presently exists. In their typically skeptical stance, they might question whether there is even smoke at all, but rather a fog, a cloud descended to earth, or an artifact of blurry vision. In this commentary on Sheldrake's contribution, I will attempt to clarify whether a valid and reliable staring detection process might indeed exist — as a true fire generating all of this smoke or, at least, as some smoldering embers — and offer suggestions about its nature.

Although Sheldrake uses the term 'the sense of being stared at', I will substitute the term *staring detection*. The latter is less awkward, and it does not contain the suggestion that a *sense* is involved. The term *sense* suggests a sensory process that staring detection might not involve. If sense is used as a synonym for *feeling*, this usually is most appropriate, in that staring detection often does involve such a subjective feeling, and it also is often accompanied by physiological indicators (e.g., tingling, burning, pressure, hair standing on end) that reflect feelings. However, it is possible for the phenomenon to involve what might better be termed a form of *direct knowing*, rather than a sensing or feeling. In still other cases, *behavioural reactions* might betray the presence of staring detection — with or without accompanying conscious awareness of the staring aspect itself.

In responding to Sheldrake's papers, I organize my remarks into five categories. These will treat the possible fictional, physical (including physiological), perceptual (chiefly visual), and attentional/intentional aspects of the staring detection process, as well as the implications of staring detection studies.

I: Is Staring Detection a Fiction?

Sheldrake begins his contribution by indicating how staring detection has been reported in lived experience surveys, treated in fictional stories and novels, and described by police officers, surveillance personnel, soldiers, hunters, photographers, and television personalities. It would be of great interest to study such field reports more carefully and in greater detail. In addition to such anecdotal reports, however, Sheldrake reviews a not insubstantial number of careful laboratory investigations of staring detection. After reviewing the research evidence that Sheldrake and others have collected, one cannot doubt that staring detection is a real and replicable phenomenon. Statistically significant staring detection effects have been repeatedly observed in Sheldrake's own research and in studies he has conducted with, or prompted in, others. Several meta-analyses have indicated the validity and reliability of staring detection (e.g. Schlitz & Braud, 1997; Schmidt et al., 2004). In short, careful research has supported the conclusion that the staring detection effect is not fictional. It can even be pointed out that Sheldrake's analyses of the reality of staring detection in his own studies are conservative ones. This is because Sheldrake's use of nonparametric tests such as chi-square and sign tests on nominal data do not consider the strengths of his obtained effects, as would analyses based on ordinal, interval, or ratio scores. Of course, not every experiment yields positive outcomes. This is to be expected of a complex human phenomenon that would likely be influenced by individual differences, predispositions, history, set, and setting.

II: Is Staring Detection a Product of Physical or Other Artifacts?

Given that it has been shown that persons are able to accurately indicate when they are being started at, by someone out of the visual range of the staree, the next step is to determine whether such accurate detection might or might not be contaminated by conventional artifacts or confounding variables such as coincidence, sensory cues (subtle sounds or other physical cues), or biases in the experimental designs. The analyses of Sheldrake and others indicate that such confounding factors can be ruled out as sources of the obtained effects. For example, sensory cues can be ruled out by having the starer and staree adequately shielded from each other through the use of one-way mirror staring or closed circuit television staring. Appropriate statistical analyses effectively rule out correct guesses attributable to 'chance coincidence'. Sheldrake addresses well and properly dismisses suggested methodological artifacts such as reporting bias and staring/nonstaring period scheduling in experiments that might introduce systematic biases that could mimic a real staring detection effect. Particularly useful are Sheldrake's observations that the initial findings of sceptical replicators of this work tend to be positive. Sheldrake convincingly argues that the sceptics then reexamine their data in attempts to explain away their positive findings. More trenchant still is Sheldrake's indictment of sceptics who postulate hypothetical processes or changes in their or others' data that might simulate real staring detection effects without demonstrating effectively that such processes or changes really have occurred. Sheldrake is careful to address studies in which possible artifacts have not been adequately controlled (e.g., the so-called NEMO tests), and he properly describes such results as suggestive only.

Additional evidence indicative of real staring effects, as opposed to artifactual ones, are the significant *correlations* that have been found between staring detection accuracy and scoring on personality tests and similar standardized assessments administered to starees. Such correlations have been found in studies by

Braud *et al.* (1993b) and by sceptic Susan Blackmore's student, Jonathan Jones (unpublished thesis, 1996).

III: Is Staring Detection a Perceptual (Chiefly Visual) Process?

Throughout the two Parts of his contribution, Sheldrake appears to treat staring detection as a perceptual — i.e., visual — process, in which the starer somehow 'reaches out and touches' the staree. This sort of spatial model/metaphor is an obvious first interpretation, given the circumstances and belief contexts in which this phenomenon originally was, and continues to be, observed. Such a view, however, does not plausibly account for laboratory findings that staring detection can successfully occur when the staree if viewed *indirectly*, via one-way mirrors or via closed circuit television. In such cases, it seems more appropriate to conclude that staring detection may be one of many manifestations of the causal efficacy of remote *attention* and *intention* (treated below). Also, the resultants of visual and other perceptual processes are definite subjective experiences; usually, these are specific and clear. Although such subjective experiences — albeit sometimes relatively vague ones — often accompany staring detection, this is not invariably the case. Staring detection can be indicated by physiological (especially autonomic) or behavioural (movements, turnings) reactions of which the staree might be unaware or only vaguely aware. Such reactions may be indicative of a form of knowing or a sensitivity that would seem to fit the outcome of remote attention or intention more closely than that of a visual or other *perceptual* process.

In my view, an interpretation that posits a kind of reaching out and touching process indicates a general discomfort with action at a distance. Just as nature abhors a vacuum, so, too, does human intellection and understanding abhor seeming *gaps* in observed phenomena. We are strongly disposed to fill such gaps with bridging, continuously connecting processes such as material substances, channels, and 'energies'; and it is tempting to attempt to do this with respect to staring detection. There are, of course, cases in which action at a distance now is accepted as a truism in several areas of conventional, relativistic, and quantum physics, although such actions were vigorously opposed when first suggested. The positing of fields is one approach to explaining some instances of action at a distance. Sheldrake's own notions of morphic or morphogenetic fields illustrate such an attempt. In cases of more conventionally recognized fields (such as gravitational and electromagnetic fields), however, the presence and strengths of such fields can be indicated mathematically and the fields can be operationally detected. One wonders what the notion of a morphic or morphogenetic field really adds, in an explanatory sense, if such fields cannot be detected, operationalized, or characterized apart from reactions or outcomes that such fields are invented to account for in the first place. Are such fields truly explanations or simply renamings of already observed outcomes and of things to be explained?

IV: Is Staring Detection an Indicator of the Efficacy
of Remote Attention and Intention?

Staring at another person is one way of paying attention to that person. Often, this attention is mixed with a specific intention — perhaps getting the other person's attention, an attempt to make contact with the person, or some other motivated observation. It is possible that such instances of strong, focused attention and/or intention may be sufficient to induce staring detection or 'the sense of being stared at' *whether or not looking or staring actually occurs.*

In our own laboratory research (Braud *et al.*, 1993a,b), we began studying staring detection because of our curiosity about whether remote attention alone might be accompanied by distinctive physiological reactions of the remote object of such attention. We had been conducting studies in which we had found that specific, directional intentions of one person — e.g., intentions or wishes to calm or activate — were accompanied by those intended reactions in remotely situated other persons (Braud & Schlitz, 1989; 1991; Radin *et al.*, 1995; Schlitz & Braud, 1997). We recognized that in these experiments, the influencer's *intention* (for a specific physiological and subjective change) was mixed with her or his *attention* (i.e., paying attention to the person whom one wished to remotely influence). So, we designed experiments in which one person simply attended to another, remotely situated other person, without intending for any particular reaction in the latter. In these experiments, one person watched the image of the remote person on a closed circuit television monitor as a way of focusing attention on the remotely situated person during certain periods, compared to other periods in which attention was not deployed in this manner. We used measures of sympathetic autonomic nervous system activity (skin conductance reactions) as a measure of the detection of this increased attention by the 'target' person. As Sheldrake indicated in his contribution, and as in other similar studies, we obtained evidence for successful autonomic staring detection in these studies (Braud *et al.*, 1993a,b). Several meta-analyses of these, and similar, experiments have indicated the significance and reliability of such studies (e.g., Schlitz & Braud, 1997; Schmidt *et al.*, 2004).

As a relatively pure test of the relative contributions of physical staring versus attention alone, a comparative experiment readily could be conducted. In such a study, persons would stare (via closed circuit television) versus not stare at others, whose physiological reactions would be monitored during multiple staring and nonstaring periods. In another part of the study, persons would strongly focus attention or not, upon physiologically monitored persons, but would do this without actually staring at the TV monitor images of the 'target' persons. The study could be extended even further by including four types of conditions: physical staring with no (or minimal) attention (this could be accomplished by a more passive form of staring, which would involve very nonmotivated, 'witnessing' looking); strong, focused attention but without physical staring; both staring and attention; and neither staring nor attention. Comparing results for the various conditions could greatly illuminate the roles of (physical) staring and (psychological) attention in staring detection experiments.

Additionally, the variability of results in staring studies — both across different investigators and at different times and circumstances within the work of a given investigator — seems more consistent with an attentional/intentional interpretation than with a physically effective staring interpretation, in that physical staring would be expected to be rather straightforward and consistent across many experiments, whereas great variations might be expected in the ability of starees, starers, and investigators to strongly and consistently focus their attentional and intentional skills in these experiments.

In still other experiments bearing on attention, we have found evidence that it is possible for persons to facilitate the attention (in the form of concentration on some centering object) of other, distantly situated persons, through deploying their own attention in a similar 'distant helping' manner (Braud et al., 1995).

In all of the above, we are interpreting staring, intention, and attention as having *causal efficacy* in actively producing changes in distant persons. Such an interpretation, of course, can be qualified by the possibility that what we are witnessing in all of these experiments is the appropriately aligned simultaneous co-arising of the staring/intention/attention activities of the starers and the reactions of the starees, in ways that have been conceptualized as *synchronicity* (by Carl Jung and his followers) or as *dependent origination* (by those within various Buddhist traditions).

V: What Are the Implications of Staring Detection Findings?

The experimental results of Sheldrake and others indicate that accurate detection of an unseen gaze (called *staring detection* in this article) is an ability that seems to be relatively widespread in the human population. As in the case of other abilities or skills, this staring detection skill may be present to varying degrees. Differences found across various studies might be attributed to differences in the sensitivity of the starees and to differences in the staring skills of starers. These differences, in turn, may be due to differences in the abilities of starers and starees, alike, to fully deploy their attentional and intentional processes.

In the most general sense, the positive outcomes of studies of this kind extend our appreciation of the range of our human potentials and of the exceptional experiences and abilities of which we are capable, which cannot be explained adequately by the constructs, theories, and worldviews of conventional science. The studies suggest a profound interconnectedness among the participants in such studies. This interconnectedness, in turn, has important implications for our understanding of our full nature, as humans, and of the range and limits of the consciousness-mediated influences that we may exert on one another. In the view of the present writer, the most important of the consciousness-related processes implicated in the staring detection effect are the fundamental ones of attention and intention. Studies addressing a variety of forms of attention and intention, in connection with staring detection, can readily be designed and conducted, and such studies should greatly expand and illuminate our understanding of this curious effect and of the nature of consciousness itself. Perhaps the most important implication of staring detection findings for consciousness studies are their indications that, under certain conditions, consciousness may have nonlocal aspects.

I began this article with an allusion to folk psychology. I think this allusion is apropos in an additional way — in terms of Sheldrake's ongoing championing, in many of his writings, of a popularization or democratization of psychology, research, and of science itself. He has done this by urging research on commonly experienced, albeit unusual, processes and phenomena, and by encouraging research by students and by members of the general public. Such more democratized inquiry can serve to complement and balance the typically exclusionary versions of research and inquiry practiced by professionals. Such an approach might encourage a greater interest in, and participation, in consciousness studies and in science and disciplined inquiry in general.

References

Braud, W.G. (2000), 'Wellness implications of retroactive intentional influence: Exploring an outrageous hypothesis', *Alternative Therapies in Health and Medicine*, **6** (1), pp. 37–48.

Braud, W.G. & Schlitz, M.J. (1989), 'A methodology for the objective study of transpersonal imagery', *Journal of Scientific Exploration*, **3**, pp. 43–63.

Braud, W.G. & Schlitz, M. J. (1991), 'Consciousness interactions with remote biological systems: Anomalous intentionality effects', *Subtle Energies: An Interdisciplinary Journal of Energetic and Informational Interactions*, **2**, pp. 1–46.

Braud, W., Shafer, D. & Andrews, S. (1993a), 'Reactions to an unseen gaze (remote attention): A review, with new data on autonomic staring detection', *Journal of Parapsychology*, **57** (4), pp. 373–90.

Braud, W., Shafer, D. & Andrews, S. (1993b), 'Further studies of autonomic detection of remote staring: Replication, new control procedures, and personality correlates', *Journal of Parapsychology*, **57** (4), pp. 391–409.

Braud, W.G., Shafer, D., McNeill, K. & Guerra, V. (1995), 'Attention focusing facilitated through remote mental interaction', *Journal of the American Society for Psychical Research*, **89** (2), pp. 103–15.

Radin, D.I., Taylor, R.K., & Braud, W.G. (1995), 'Remote mental influence of human electrodermal activity: A pilot replication', *European Journal of Parapsychology*, **11**, pp. 19–34.

Schlitz, M. & Braud, W.G. (1997), 'Distant intentionality and healing: Assessing the evidence', *Alternative Therapies*, **3** (6), pp. 62–73.

Schmidt, S, Schneider, R., Utts, J. & Walach, H. (2004), 'Distant intentionality and the feeling of being stared at: Two meta-analyses', *British Journal of Psychology*, **95**, pp. 235–47.

JEAN E. BURNS

Detection of Staring — Psi or Statistical Artifact?

I will first discuss the evidence for detection of staring given in Part 1 of Sheldrake's paper and then add a brief comment on the theory proposed in his Part 2.

The term *detection of staring* refers to the ability to be aware that another person is staring at you, without any means of detection by sensory perception or any means whatever that can be described by presently known physical laws. This means that detection of staring is an aspect of psi, the latter being the general name for phenomena that take place in accord with mental intention and cannot be accounted for by those laws. It is, of course, possible that an addition or extension to known physical laws could be made which takes into account the action of consciousness. Presently known physical laws were never intended to describe consciousness, but only matter. And the history of physics shows that radical additions to physics are sometimes made as new phenomena are taken into account. Nevertheless, if psi is real, a radical extension of physical laws, which takes into account the action of consciousness, would have to be made (Burns, 2003). So evidence for psi need not be considered conclusive if some alternative explanation which falls within the purview of presently known laws can reasonably be offered.

One possibility that could offer such an explanation is that of bias matching. This can occur if the target sequence is not properly randomized. In more detail, the starer is given a sequence of instructions, *stare* or *not stare*, with said list supposedly randomized. The staree then produces a sequence of responses, *stare* or *not stare*, according to his impression at the appropriate times. However, as is known by numerous experiments, if a person is asked to produce a sequence of binary choices, such a sequence is apt to be patterned, not random (Brugger and Taylor, 2003). Such sequences are especially apt to show *alternation bias*, i.e., they will show fewer doubles, triples, and higher n-tuples than a random sequence would, and therefore have more alternation from one choice to another than a random sequence. So if the target sequence happens also to have alternation bias, these sequences can match up (Brugger and Taylor, 2003). The effect will look like psi, but has an ordinary explanation.

As Sheldrake reports (p. 24), target sequences he had used from his website had been randomized with respect to other considerations, but not with respect to alternation bias. Colwell *et al.* (2000) analysed the first 12 sequences from that perspective. If these 12 sequences (of 20 targets each) had been random, they should have had a total of 114 two-element repetitions; there actually were 89. There should have been 54 same-element three-tuples; there were 22. There should have been 25.5 same-element four-tuples; there were 4. And so forth.

Colwell *et al.* (2000) used these sequences to perform the same experiments Sheldrake had done. When target-by-target feedback was given, participants performed at higher than chance level. However, this could be interpreted as a matching of the bias in the target sequence with the alternation bias of the staree, so this result need not be attributed to psi.

Sheldrake (p. 21) notes that pattern matching through implicit learning could account for above-chance results in his experiments with feedback, and he quite properly does not offer these results as conclusive evidence for the staring effect. However, Colwell *et al.* (2000) reported that a learning effect took place in their experiments with feedback — each successive block of three sequences showed improvement in detection of staring, but detection of non-staring remained at chance — and Sheldrake (p. 24) asserts that implicit learning could not account for this contrast between staring and non-staring sequences. But a staree might have a preferential interest in the *yes* response and, with feedback, use implicit learning (rather than psi) to preferentially improve his response to that part of the target pattern. So the learning effect does not establish the existence of staring detection either.

Sheldrake (p. 21) asserts that pattern matching in the sequences could not take place without feedback and offers the experiments described in Sheldrake (2000), done without feedback, as evidence for the staring effect. However, the question of whether pattern matching can take place in the absence of feedback deserves a little more examination.

None of the sequences — target or human response generated — would have alternations which go on indefinitely. Sometimes an element will repeat, or there will be a triple or quadruple, and even-numbered repetitions put the new alternation out of phase with the previous one. If a set of response alternations is matched to a set of target alternations, and one set changes phase, the responses will now be mismatched. When there is feedback, there apparently is a tendency for the response sequence to go back in phase. So the target matching is higher than chance. Without feedback it would seem that the alternation portions of the target and response sequences go in and out of phase, with no net result.

Colwell et al. (2000) did Sheldrake's staring experiment without feedback, using the above-described 12 sequences with alternation bias, and found chance results. This supports the idea that even when target and response sequences are both biased, without feedback there is no net matching. Sheldrake (2000) got above-chance results with no feedback, which he claims is evidence for the staring effect. He ascribes the chance results of Colwell et al. to the experimenter effect, i.e., that some experimenters produce psi more readily than others (Smith, 2003).

However, questions remain. For one thing Sheldrake (2000) reported that the experiments used 24 sequences, which suggests that he used the 24 sequences on his website that turned out to have defective randomization. If a target sequence is susceptible to bias matching with feedback, it is possible that a matching effect might also take place without it. So the above-chance results in these experiments do not confirm the existence of the staring effect.

This brings us to the question of what sort of randomization is needed for a staring experiment. Colwell et al. (2000) reviewed various randomization procedures and concluded that specific testing of target sequences for same-element n-tuple deficits should be done. In a second set of experiments they used 10 new target sequences of 20 binary digits each which were derived from a random number table. They tested for deficits in two- and three-tuple same-element repetitions and found the sequences satisfactory. A staring experiment with feedback using these sequences provided chance results, and they concluded that the difference from the earlier experiments with feedback, which gave an above-chance result, was the lesser degree of structure in the new sequences. However, there does not seem to presently be any standard procedure to ensure against alternation bias in target sequences.

There is also the question of what sort of matching biases could occur in the absence of feedback. Brugger and Taylor (2003) suggest that if the first element of the response sequence can be correlated to the target sequence, a matching bias can be produced. On the other hand, Palmer (1996) investigated the possibility that local patterning within a random target sequence could match with patterns in a response sequence to give a net matching effect. He found, for the well-randomized target sequences he investigated, there was no significant effect.

It would seem reasonable to randomize target sequences sufficiently to guard against possible matching with biases in response sequences, even when there is no feedback. However, response biases can vary according to personality type and other variables (Brugger and Taylor, 2003), so guarding against possible matching is not a matter of dealing solely with alternation bias. At present there is no agreement as to what randomization procedures should be used.

As we have seen, Sheldrake's experiments done with feedback cannot be used to demonstrate the existence of the staring effect because the target sequences were not sufficiently randomized to guard against alternation matching. And the experiments reported in Sheldrake (2000) cannot be used to demonstrate its existence because (a) the target sequences might not have been randomized against alternation bias and (b) not enough is known about what randomization procedures can guard against bias matching in general to make a definitive proof. Sheldrake also asserts that parapsychology experiments using closed circuit television (CCTV) and recording the subjects' skin resistance can confirm the existence of the staring effect. Let's examine this question next.

There are two types of parapsychology experiments which are relevant to the staring effect. One is called *remote staring*. In this experiment the agent (starer) and receiver (staree) are in two separated rooms, well insulated from any sensory communication. Once they are in these rooms, the agent follows a sequence of stare, non-stare instructions. He can view the receiver on CCTV, and for a stare instruction the agent stares at the image of the receiver on the monitor. For a non-stare instruction the agent looks in some other direction and thinks of something else. There are rest periods between instructions. The electrodermal activity (EDA) of the subject is recorded continuously throughout the session. When the trials are done, the EDA for the stare periods is compared with the EDA for the non-stare periods, and a statistically significant difference between these results would indicate the presence of psi.

The other relevant type of parapsychology experiment is called Direct Mental Interaction with Living Systems (DMILS). This experiment is very similar to remote staring experiments. However, the agent's instructions are to have the intention to either activate or calm the autonomic nervous system of the receiver. And instead of the agent's viewing the receiver on a monitor, he views the ongoing record of the receiver's EDA.

The remote staring experiments show a difference in EDA between the staring and non-staring conditions, and the DMILS experiments show a difference between the calm and activate conditions. It would seem that these experiments, with their extensive shielding of any ordinary sensory communication and use of a physiological measure of the activity of the autonomic nervous system, could resolve the issue of whether detection of staring and DMILS exist. However, recent studies have shown that the methods used to measure the EDA in these experiments were not completely up to date with current psychophysiological methods (Schmidt *et al.*, 2001; Schmidt and Walach, 2000). So a recent meta-analysis has concluded that while past experiments hint at the possibility of these psi effects, further experiments using high quality methods are needed before any definite conclusions could be drawn (Schmidt *et al.*, 2004).

In summary, Sheldrake's work, while interesting and suggestive, does not establish the existence of the detection of staring phenomenon. As we have just seen, parapsychology experiments have not established the existence of this phenomenon either. It remains an interesting possibility, but only that.

In Part 2 Sheldrake points out that even if a phenomenon is not established, one can go ahead and theorize about it. Certainly this is so, but Sheldrake seeks to make his theory of morphic fields explain a large number of things, not all of which need any explanation beyond the physical principles we already know. For instance, he asserts that his theory can explain protein folding. However, while it is difficult to predict the three-dimensional configuration of proteins, this is because a folded protein consists of a long ribbon which is held in its configuration because of numerous interactions between parts on neighbouring strands (Creighton, 1994). There is no reason to think the shape of a folded protein cannot be explained by ordinary physical laws.

On the other hand, Sheldrake proposes his theory as an explanation for detection of staring, a form of psi. If psi is real, its explanation must assuredly be different than known physical laws (Burns, 2003). In this respect, Sheldrake's proposals can be viewed as a theory of psi.

References

Brugger, P. and Taylor, K.I. (2003), 'ESP: Extrasensory perception or effect of subjective probability?', *Journal of Consciousness Studies*, **10** (6–7), pp. 221–46.

Burns, J.E. (2003), 'What is beyond the edge of the known world?', *Journal of Consciousness Studies*, **10** (6–7), pp. 7–28.

Colwell, J., Schröder, S. and Sladen, D. (2000), 'The ability to detect unseen staring: A literature review and empirical tests', *British Journal of Psychology*, **91**, pp. 71–85.

Creighton, T.E. (1994), 'The protein folding problem', in *Mechanisms of Protein Folding*, ed. R.H. Pain (Oxford: Oxford University Press).

Palmer, J. (1996), 'Evaluation of a conventional interpretation of Helmut Schmidt's automated precognition experiments', *Journal of Parapsychology*, **60**, pp. 149–70.

Schmidt, S., Schneider, R., Binder, M., Bürkle, D. and Walach, H. (2001), 'Investigating methodological issues in EDA-DMILS: Results from a pilot study', *Journal of Parapsychology*, **65**, pp. 59-82.

Schmidt, S., Schneider, R., Utts, J. and Walach, H. (2004), 'Distant intentionality and the feeling of being stared at: Two meta-analyses', *British Journal of Psychology*, **95**, pp. 235–47.

Schmidt, S. and Walach, H. (2000), 'Electrodermal activity (EDA) — state-of-the-art measurement and techniques for parapsychological purposes', *Journal of Parapsychology*, **64**, pp. 139–63.

Sheldrake, R. (2000), 'The "sense of being stared at" does not depend on known sensory clues', *Rivista di Biologia/Biology Forum*, **93**, pp. 237–52.

Smith, M.D. (2003), 'The role of the experimenter in parapsychological research', *Journal of Consciousness Studies*, **10** (6–7), pp. 69–84.

R.H.S. CARPENTER

Does Scopesthesia Imply Extramission?

The fact that an opinion has been widely held is no evidence whatever that it is not utterly absurd; indeed in view of the silliness of the majority of mankind, a widespread belief is more likely to be foolish than sensible.
— Bertrand Russell, *Marriage and Morals* (1929)

The most savage controversies are those about matters as to which there is no good evidence either way ... Whenever you find yourself getting angry about a difference of opinion, be on your guard; you will probably find, on examination, that your belief is going beyond what the evidence warrants.
— Bertrand Russell, *An Outline of Intellectual Rubbish* (1950)

Nothing is better calculated to enrage a right-thinking scientist than popular belief in a phenomenon whose existence cannot quite be disproved, but which if true must bring into question the most fundamental axioms on which the scientific description of the world is constructed. The existence of a sense that one is being looked at — one might perhaps call it *scopesthesia*, which is briefer and sounds more scientific — is just such a belief. It is indeed popular. As Sheldrake says, 'most people have had the experience of turning round, feeling that someone is looking at them from behind, and finding this is the case' (p. 10): I have myself, quite often. However, I also know how very fallible my perceptions can be. Invariably, sitting in a stationary train when a neighbouring train moves off, I think it is me that is moving. When I see the moon near the horizon it looks twice as big as normal. I am a sucker for every kind of geometrical illusion — Müller-Lyer, Poggendorf, Zöllner — the lot. And as a professional psychophysicist I know very well how little correspondence there can be between even one's strongest perceptual convictions, and what is actually the case.

Rupert Sheldrake is also well aware of these problems, and it is very much to his credit that he has made this attempt to assemble the kind of statistical evidence that is needed to convince scientists of the reality of scopesthesia. It is not his fault that he comes to this task with a personal conviction that the phenomenon exists: there can be very few scientists who do not have strong hopes and fears about the outcome of their experiments. And it is not his fault that some of the evidence that he brings forward is so very weak: although the nature of the Bayesian process that underlies scientific experimentation is that all evidence, whether weak or strong, is cumulative, nevertheless evidence that is feeble, or too tendentiously interpreted, has a strongly negative psychological effect, and he might more judiciously, if less conscientiously, have passed over it in silence.

So what does this evidence, in the end, amount to? Two inter-related phenomena are considered: (a) the sense of being looked at that is confirmed on turning round, and (b) the ability to cause people to feel looked at, and consequently to turn round, simply by looking at them. Clearly (b) is the stronger of the two in the sense that if it could be convincingly demonstrated it would provide a complete explanation for (a); on the other hand (a) on its own could be explained in many ways that would not violate current scientific orthodoxy, as Titchener pointed out over a century ago. It may be that subjects tend to recollect those occasions when their scopesthesia was confirmed, and forget those when it wasn't. In addition, the act of turning round is very likely to attract the gaze of someone behind: since it takes about a second to turn one's head but the latency of a saccade is only about a fifth of a second, the viewee is more likely than not to find the viewer looking at them. Thus the popularity of the belief in (a) — undoubtedly widespread, as Sheldrake convincingly illustrates — provides only the weakest of evidence.

What about (b), the ability to induce scopesthesia by actively looking at someone? Sheldrake again adduces a quantity of anecdotal information, open as always to the criticism that favourable events are better remembered than unfavourable. But here at least there is the possibility of what a scientist would recognise as a proper controlled experiment. We need to eliminate those unsupervised tests where cheating was possible, those where individual participants could choose whether to contribute their results or not, those where covert cues could have been transmitted, and those where the experiments are insufficiently described to be able to evaluate them. From Sheldrake's list, and using his very fair assessments of their value, it appears we are then left with just five published experiments (Coover, 1913; Poortman, 1959; Williams, 1983; Marks and Colwell, 2001; Wiseman and Smith, 1995 — see Sheldrake's list of references for details). Of these, three gave negative results. Since there are many ways in which artefactual correlations can arise in such experiments, but rather few that can result in masking of a genuine effect, and bearing in mind that a positive result is more likely to be considered worth publishing, it is difficult for an unbiased enquirer not to conclude that scopesthesia is an illusion.

But Sheldrake clearly feels otherwise, and the second part of his paper is a description of a theory of vision that he believes to be a necessary consequence of the existence of scopesthesia. It is that vision is not simply the result of a one-way flow of information from the observed object to the brain; there are 'perceptual fields that link the observer to that which is perceived ... rooted in the brain but [extending] far beyond it' (p. 32). As with scopesthesia itself, Sheldrake attaches much importance to popular (and ancient) belief, in this case that vision is something that proceeds from the eye out into the real world — 'extramission' — rather than vice-versa. We are told (p. 37) that 80% of a group of children in Ohio agreed that vision involved 'rays, energy or something else' being sent out from the eyes — and for good measure, 75% of them said they could 'feel the stares of other people'. This less than compelling piece of evidence — in the same vein, I would predict (and Amazon might confirm) that those who believe in crystal healing also tend to believe in astrology — is reinforced by a long account of pre-scientific philosophers who professed a similar belief.

This notion is meant to solve what in conventional neuroscience Sheldrake seems to regard as an intolerable *reductio ad absurdam*: that when one looks at an elephant, the elephant is in some sense inside one's head. How can this be? Obviously, most would reply, because in some *other* sense the elephant is actually projected on to the outside world; the apparent contradiction need worry us no more than the fact that the retinal image of the elephant is upside-down. But on this pseudo-paradox Sheldrake erects a shaky edifice of 'perceptual fields, extending out beyond the brain ... fields of probability ... [resembling] the fields of quantum field theory' (pp. 42, 44). Inevitably, Schrödinger's cat is dragged out of his box, the mantra of quantum entanglement of observer and observed is intoned, and one mysterious phenomenon is 'explained' by another.

Of course Sheldrake understands perfectly well the unsatisfactory flimsiness of all this, and admits that such 'speculations ... are still vague' (p. 48); his defence is that neuroscientific explanations of the consciousness of qualia are equally vague, and I would absolutely agree with him. If incontrovertible evidence could be found that scopesthesia actually existed, then that would indeed rule out a number of 'scientific' theories of consciousness; but no such experimental support exists. Over-hyping weak evidence — as recent political events have shown — does not always have the effect that is intended.

CHRIS CLARKE

The Sense of Being Stared At:
Its Relevance to the Physics of Consciousness

In my response I am taking it that Rupert Sheldrake has established a *prima facie* case for this phenomenon, and I focus on his second — theoretical — paper, where he proposes that the sense of being stared at involves a process in which 'projection [of the perceptual visual image onto the external object] takes place through perceptual fields' (p. 42). The phenomenon thus concerns consciousness studies because it is connected with a process of projection which many authors see as central to the production of the visual content of conscious awareness. I agree with a core aspect of this idea; but, as I shall argue below, I do not think that Sheldrake's notion of 'field' adds anything helpful to this core aspect.

An essential issue here is the nature of the 'projection', in which a perceptual image or representation of the perceived object is formed by processing in the brain, but then is located not in the brain but in a space extending out beyond the skull to the external world. Sheldrake cites Velmans, in particular, as using the term 'projection' in consciousness studies. Now, if this projection is a purely physical function of the perceptual system, then we are in danger of falling into precisely the same regress that Sheldrake rightly criticises in the case of the 'Cartesian Theatre', in which the brain forms an *internal* projected image which is then viewed by some kind of homunculus inside the brain. Whether the projection is internal or external, if it is purely physical then we still have the problem of who or what then perceives it in order for it to enter consciousness — potentially leading to an infinite regress. Velmans steers well clear of this danger because for him 'projection' is very much a metaphor, and the image is a strictly non-physical construction within a conscious perceptual space that lines up with physical space but is distinct from it.

For Sheldrake the projection has, it would seem, to be both physical and perceptual. It has to be perceptual in order to avoid the regress of the Cartesian Theatre, but also physical in order to be a field (distributed in physical space and interacting with other fields) and to convey an influence to another person. His proposal is thus a kind of dual aspect theory in which the perceptual field (if not other systems) has both physical and mental (or noetic) aspects. The perceptual field links the starer and the staree into a single physical system that is itself possessed of consciousness. The conscious aspect, when focused down onto the starer, becomes the perception of staring; and when focused down onto the staree become the perception of being stared at. This is the core idea that I find promising. Three issues arising from this must then, however, be addressed.

I: Why is the Perceptual Field Necessary for Consciousness in Visual Perception?

On the conventional view of vision, the perceiver and the object of perception are already linked together by an electromagnetic interaction (normally construed as one-way), so that they are no longer self-contained systems, but need to be considered as a whole. Suppose that we adopt a dual aspect view of this system, just as Sheldrake adopts a dual aspect view of the perceptual field. If consciousness is one of two aspects of such a combined system, then the object (or rather, aspects of it) will be part of this consciousness, *associated with the place of the object*, and it will be joined with a self-consciousness of the subject. These together will constitute the conscious perception of the object without the need for any projection or any further field. In a view such as this, the role of the information-processing system of the brain is to establish a physical (but one-way) link between specifically selected aspects of an external object and some particular subsystem of the brain associated with the 'I' of the perceiver.

The only thing added, in the case of ordinary vision, by doubling up the fields with a perceptual field in addition to the electromagnetic field, is an explanation of the subjective feeling that vision is somehow active. But that feeling is already explained by the fact that vision is indeed active: unlike the exposure of a photograph, it involves the complex activity of attention and analysis that Sheldrake himself describes.

In the case of staring, as far as the general contents of consciousness is concerned, the account just given seems adequate also to explain the sense of being stared at without the use of a further field. Just as the consciousness possessed by this joint system, when reduced to the starer, gives the perception of seeing, so, when reduced to the staree, it might give the perception of being stared at. At this level of generality, once a single system is established by an electromagnetic interaction, then no further sort of interaction seems required, either for normal vision or for the sense of being stared at. For the latter, however, an additional problem arises which I consider next.

II: How Is Information Transmitted?

It would seem that the only deficiency of an electromagnetic interaction for the staring phenomenon is that, in this case, it can only convey information in one direction: the back-reaction from the eye of the perceiver to the neck of the perceived is so minute as to be completely ignorable. (This remains the case with the Wheeler-Feynman theory considered by Sheldrake, which is designed to reproduce precisely the phenomena of ordinary electromagnetic theory, including unidirectional information flow.) Another field, going in the other direction, thus seems to be needed to explain the informational content of the sense of being stared at. But note that this move is now only a device to account for the *physical* fact of information flow in a parapsychology experiment and is not required as part of the theory of consciousness or of the theory of vision. It is thus not the case that the hypothesis of perceptual fields economically explains separate problems in parapsychology, vision and consciousness studies. Once reduced to the level of information flow, the elaborate series of properties assigned to the perceptual field in this paper seem to be doing no more than re-describing the phenomenon in other words, rather than explaining it, a point on which I enlarge in the next section.

I should add here that none of the quantum mechanical theories cited by Sheldrake overcome this problem of the direction of information flow, even though at first glance they seem to imply an action of the perceiver on the perceived. My own theory (Clarke, 2004), for example, considers the perceiver and the perceived to be entangled systems. But here it is well known that information cannot normally be conveyed between entangled systems without the existence of a parallel non-quantum channel of information flow.[9] Admittedly the situation might be different in my theory because of its unconventional starting point. Following Whitehead, I consider a picture where pure states are regarded as the primary conscious elements in the universe and decoherence is held at bay by the Zeno effect of self-observation. Whether or not this circumvents the impossibility of communicating information through entanglement alone remains to be established, but it seems a long shot.

III: What Is a 'Field'?

Sheldrake proposes that 'the perceptual projection is not just analogous to but actually is a field phenomenon' (p. 42). It would seem, therefore, that he has something quite specific in mind when using the word 'field', and that his concept of field is intended to have explanatory power rather than being merely descriptive of the phenomenon itself. To clarify this, let us compare the situation here with that of the magnetic field. At first this latter concept was merely descriptive: the magnetic field was a propensity, manifest at every point in space, for a compass needle to point in a particular direction. This was not a theory but merely a form of words describing the phenomenon. The situation changed

---

[9] A useful introduction to the quantum information theory involved here, including many references, can be found at http://www.imaph.tu-bs.de/qi/concepts.html

radically when it was noted that the magnetic field was governed by a simple law: that the flux of the field into any closed surface was precisely balanced by the flux out of that surface (or any of the equivalent versions of this statement). This immediately led to a host of predictions which could be tested, thereby moving from a description to a (partial) explanation.

I suggest that the term 'field', if it is to be explanatory and at all analogous to the situation with classical fields, needs to denote an entity that (a) is extended in space and has distinctive attributes at each point, and (b) is subject to some sort of law-like behaviour that is simpler than the phenomena that it is to explain. In enunciating (b) I require that the law-like behaviour is expressed directly in terms of the field, and not in terms of the field's effects, because only then does the field itself become an explanatory concept.

Applying these criteria to the perceptual field, it seems to satisfy (a) in that it has, at each point, the property that any body placed at that point will enter the visual field at an appropriate position. Regarding (b) we could go on to elaborate laws for the perceptual field involving what happens to it if we interpose mirrors, prisms, lenses, etc. ... but these would be none other than the laws of optics rephrased 'in reverse', adding nothing to what we already have in conventional theory. It is clear that Sheldrake is thinking of more than this, and he enumerates further properties of the perceptual field, shared by all morphic fields, which do indeed go beyond a reformulation of optics. I cannot, however, find here anything that would lead me to use the term 'field' for the carrier of these further properties. I will conclude by explaining my difficulty in the case of the clearest examples of the properties of morphic fields. Sheldrake writes:

> First, by their nature they could connect together patterns of activity in different regions of the brain (p. 44).

I suggest that, since this holds of almost any interaction at all, it is too non-specific to be regarded as law-like for a field.

> Second, they contain attractors (p. 44).

An attractor, we recall (e.g. from Arrowsmith and Place, 1992), is a subset of the state-space of a dynamical system which has a non-trivial neighbourhood from which all trajectories approach the attractor, and which is indecomposable with respect to this property. Thus it is a property of a given dynamical system, not something which in itself specifies a dynamical system. To say that a dynamical system 'contains attractors' says almost nothing about that system. For instance, *any* dynamical system not everywhere ergodic and with a compact phase space will contain an attractor. This statement is therefore not in any way law-like. (Nor indeed is it clear, since it is ambiguous as to whether it refers to the dynamical system describing the way the field changes, or, in the particular case of a vector field, to the dynamical system generated by the field itself.)

> Third, they link into a single system the subject and the object (p. 44).

We have just noted, however, that these are already linked by existing physical fields, and by any other interaction between them, whether a field or not. We need to know the nature of the linkage to judge whether it can be called a field and whether it adds anything to the conventional picture.

Sheldrake's original picture of the morphogenetic field was indeed a field because it was subject to a law in which its strength increased with a memory effect. I suggest that this is not the case with perceptual fields, and that the concept is in need of clarification before it can seen how it explains the sense of being stared at.

References

Arrowsmith, D.K. and Place, C.M. (1992), *Dynamical Systems* (London: CRC Press).
Clarke, Chris (2004), 'Quantum mechanics, consciousness and the self', in *Science, Consciousness and Ultimate Reality,* ed. David Lorimer (Exeter: Imprint Academic).

RALPH ELLIS

The Ambiguity of 'In Here/Out There' Talk:
In What Sense Is Perception 'Out in the World'?

Sheldrake presents evidence that subjects have a slight but significant ability to detect being looked at, even when they apparently cannot 'see' the person looking at them in any traditionally understood scientific sense of 'see'. I shall leave to others the critique of his methodology, and focus on the implications of his findings. Sheldrake rejects several alternative explanations, offering instead a theory that there are perceptual fields that extend 'outside the head'. I argue that we do not need to descend to the quantum level, or abandon traditional accounts of perception, in order to accommodate the findings. The idea of perceptual fields, while possibly true, is not necessarily entailed by the phenomenon of awareness of being looked at.

I: 'Representations in the Head' and Perceptual Fields

Sheldrake emphasizes that people have an ability to detect not only being stared at from behind, but also when looked at on a TV monitor by someone in a different room. Informally, he endorses anecdotal accounts of military personnel who are aware of being stared at through telescopes or binoculars from a great distance, and he wants his theory to be able to accommodate these experiences of being stared at from a great distance, through closed doors, and *via* TV monitors. As far as the actual data are concerned, none of it would contradict such reports, and none of it suggests that the ability to detect being looked at is more pronounced at shorter distances, or even when the subject is in the same room with the looker.

Consequently, if the perceptual fields that Sheldrake characterizes as 'outside of our heads' are to account for these facts, they would have to be fields that remain very strong even at a great distance from the head. To get around this kind of problem, Sheldrake proposes a novel account of perception in terms of a theory of quantum effects in the perceived field which purportedly interact with the perceptual fields.

The move to a quantum-level hypothesis is motivated by the observed anomaly that the distance between subject and looker does not seem to affect the subject's sense of being stared at. This means that, if the quantum-level explanation is to avoid functioning as an *ad hoc* hypothesis, two conditions must be met: (1) the quantum hypothesis must be the best way to account for the anomalous findings; and (2) the overall theory about perceptual fields outside the head, which motivated the quantum hypothesis, must itself be supported by cogent arguments indicating that *it* is the most plausible approach to explaining the general phenomenon of awareness of being looked at.

The second of these two conditions is the more basic one, so let's start with it. I have some problems with Sheldrake's reasons for endorsing the perceptual fields outside the head theory. The idea that perception takes place 'outside the head' seems to be based on an ambiguous philosophical claim that 'the perceived object', 'the percept', or perception itself is 'out there in the world' rather than 'inside the head'. But in fact, the theory that there are representations 'inside the head', which bears the brunt of Sheldrake's criticisms of alternative accounts based on theories of representation, is a cartoon caricature of that type of theory, and thus a straw man. Sheldrake speaks as if traditional accounts of representation held that representations are thing-like entities or static physical structures that are literally held in some spatial location inside the head. I doubt whether *any* traditional believer in representation would posit such a simplistic account. Most, at least if they have studied much neuroscience, would grant that representing is an *activity* that the brain stands ready to execute when triggered in some way (for example, Thomas, 1989).

It is true that analytic philosophers, prior to the past decade of 'consciousness revolution', had badly mangled their accounts of what a representation is. But Natika Newton (1996; 2000; 2001; 2003; 2004) — the one 'enactivist' who has systematically provided an adequate account of representation in several different places (including those just cited) — is notably missing from Sheldrake's discussion of the enactivist alternatives. On Newton's account, representation does not mean an abstract symbolic event isomorphic to and caused by its referent, as traditionally postulated by theorists in philosophy of mind (for example, Fodor, 1975; 1987). She also does not mean purely pictorial representation, as the term 'imagery' traditionally implies. Instead, representation on her account is an activity in which we imaginatively simulate embodied sensorimotor actions toward a symbolizing element, where the isomorphism, as Merleau-Ponty (1942/1963) suggested, is between the *actions* afforded by the symbol and those afforded by what the symbol represents. That which the symbol represents, on this view, is determined not by the stimulus that originally produced it, but by the imagined actions performed upon it. Consciousness exists to help organisms unify their efforts so as to achieve goals that require long-range planning. Goals such as appeasement of hunger, whose satisfaction mechanisms are not built into the system, must be explicitly represented in such a way that the representations can activate higher-order goal-seeking activity. Just as a feeding mechanism recognizes when it has achieved a state of satiation, and when it has not, so a conscious organism requires a way of recognizing when it has achieved its more abstract goal. Lacking a hard-wired system for identifying, say, the state of having successfully completed one's PhD dissertation, we need to create a representation of that state, and then organize our multiple abilities to achieve it, and to recognize when it has been achieved. Mechanisms for mental representation are designed to make this behaviour possible, through comparison processes.

Traditional accounts of representation emphasize that the representing entity must be both isomorphic to and closely causally linked with the represented element. Neither isomorphism nor causation, of course, can make one thing represent another in a meaningful sense. As Thelen *et al.* (2001) point out, any dynamic internal event causally related to something external would then constitute a representation. Newton's position is that representation does occur — through a subject's *use* of it *in context* of embodied (organismically-purposeful) action. This formulation allows for both conscious and preconscious representation: R represents object O if, because of some appropriate isomorphism, R plays the role of O in a simulated action involving O, either consciously or preconsciously (for example, habituatedly).

Notice that, on this account, there is no need to posit that representations are fixed entities or static structures in the brain. Representing is something that we do, when triggered in the right way by purpose-defined conditions. Representations are not little physical objects inside the head. But the kind of representation Newton wants to allow for (because of the role it plays in action planning) does acknowledge that certain activities of the brain are necessary and sometimes sufficient substrates of the execution of the activities that we call imaging and representing.

We can image (and thus represent) something that exists nowhere in the world 'outside our heads'. And even when red appears to be pasted to the surface of objects, we know from a vast collection of scientific evidence that the way red looks is largely a function of the way our brains are designed to 'represent' certain collections of quantum events (actions of photons, etc.). In fact, the red is not pasted to the surface of the object, as it appears to be, but rather created by our brain activity. So to insist that the red is 'out there in the world' rather than 'in our heads' is both ambiguous and an attack on a straw man. Suppose we distinguish between things that are simply physical objects or structures existing literally 'inside the head' on the one hand, and on the other hand conditions of the brain that make it ready and able to execute the action of representing something in the way defined by Newton. Those representations are 'in the head' in a less literal and more complicated sense: they are activities of constellations of brain states that enable us to represent something when triggered. We can designate these two different senses of 'in the head' as 'ITH-1' and 'ITH-2'. So we can say that Newton's representations are ITH-2, but not ITH-1.

The most traditional theorists of perception and representation do not think that the appearance of red means that there is a red replica of the object in my head (ITH-1), or even an object that is isomorphic to the red object that is perceived. But in the richer sense of 'in the head' (ITH-2), it is true that many of the activities that create the appearance 'red' are executed by the brain, and in that sense they do take place 'inside the head'.

Sheldrake's jump from the thesis that representations or percepts are not 'in the head' to the conclusion that perceptual fields surrounding our brains must physically extend out to where the object is located is based on the very equivocation of the meaning of 'in the head' we have just been discussing. In one sense (ITH-2), the enactive execution of a representation is done *by* things in the head (brain events), but this does not in any way imply that the *intentional objects* of those representations are physical objects in the head. Husserl (1900/1913; 1913/1931) and the other classic phenomenologists are very careful to make and clarify the distinction between physical objects and intentional objects as they appear to us, as well as to acknowledge that there are psychophysical relations between them (Husserl, 1962). The phenomenologists are certainly quite clear in spelling out that what is meant by an 'intentional object' of a conscious act is *not* a little physical replica of any object inside the head; but Husserl is also well aware that this account of intentionality is perfectly consistent with various alternative accounts of the ways in which specific brain functions are needed to subserve the intentional acts executed by conscious subjects.

II: The Realm of Alternative Explanations

There is a set of alternative possible explanations of phenomena like the awareness of being stared at when not mediated by direct perception. Ironically, Sheldrake's preferred 'perceptual fields' theory, with its accompanying hypothesis about quantum interactions with the field, falls within the set of possible alternative explanations. What is needed is some way for a subject to gain awareness of its environment in some way other than through direct perception. In my view, Occam's razor would suggest that we do not commit ourselves to new theories if an equally adequate explanation can be given using already tested theories.

The general class of explanations as to how awareness of being stared at could exist without perceptual mediation has been well characterized by Gendlin (1992):

> To begin philosophy by considering perception makes it seem that living things can contact reality only through perception. But plants *are* in contact with reality. They *are* interactions, quite without perception. Our own living bodies also *are* interactions with their environments, and that is not lost just because ours also have perception. . . . Our bodies . . . interact as bodies, not just through what comes with the five senses. . . .
>
> Merleau-Ponty . . . meant perception to include (latently and implicitly) also our bodily interactional being-in-the-world, all of our life in situations. . . The body senses the whole situation, and it urges, it implicitly shapes our next action. It senses itself living-in its whole context — the situation. . . .
>
> From one ancient bone one can reconstruct not only the whole animal, but from its body also the kind of environment in which it lived. . . . The body even as a dead structure still contains all that implicit information about its environment. . . .

> My warmth or hostility will affect your ongoing bodily being whether you perceive it or not. You may find it there, if you sense how your body has the situation (Gendlin, 1992, pp. 344–53).

The body is affected by its overall interrelations with the environment; so, if we sense how our bodies have changed from one moment to the next, we may be able to guess somewhat as to what kind of environmental changes may have occurred to make our bodies feel different. Such guesses may not be very accurate, because for any effect there are a variety of possible causes. But if the guess is based on the presumption simply that *something* has changed in the environment, the odds are much better. On Gendlin's type of account, we can detect when *something* has changed much better than we can detect *what* has changed. If we are given the clue that the change, if there is a change, will consist of a person looking at us from behind, then our odds of success are better, because we have the ability to feel our bodies changing, and our bodies are in interaction with the world.

Of course, one of the ways that our bodies are in interaction with the world is at the quantum level. But on Gendlin's account, the detection of the change in the body is not *perceptual*. We do not need to have vision of a person in order to have a sense that she is there. There are many ways that this can be known — for example, in the amount of carbon dioxide being replenished into the atmosphere, in the reaction of nearby animals and birds to the presence or absence of the distant person, and the list could go on and on. Many of these cues can be eliminated in carefully controlled laboratory circumstances, but we do not know how many of them there are, and thus it would be difficult to control them all.

My point is that, while the quantum apparatus of the elaborate theory of perceptual fields is a hypothesis consistent with the data, there are also other hypotheses that are consistent with it, and many of them do not require adopting entirely new theoretical proposals.

Let me conclude with a final question that would seem to present a problem for Sheldrake's explanation as well as for the entire realm of alternative explanations for these kinds of phenomena: Suppose it is true that subjects can detect being stared at on TV monitors. And suppose we set up an experiment in which twins are in separate studios. Two different lookers in different rooms, in randomized intervals, see pictures of the back of one twin's head, alternating with a view of the other's, but do not know which one they are looking at in any given moment. On Sheldrake's theory, would the twins pick up on the experience of being looked at by the incorrect looker as often as by the correct one? Or would the twin subjects be able to detect when they were the one actually being looked at? The perceptual apparatus of the lookers would presumably be exactly the same when looking at one twin or the other; and the image on the TV monitor would be exactly the same, regardless of which twin is actually represented on it. So it would seem that there is no real physical difference between being looked at oneself and having one's twin looked at. If the twins would be able to detect being looked at (and thus discriminate which twin is being looked at by which looker), there would seem to be no possible physical explanation for such an effect, since there is no physical difference between the two conditions being discriminated — being looked at oneself and having one's twin looked at.

If a subject cannot tell the difference between being looked at and having his or her twin looked at, then the subject is not really detecting when he or she is or is not being looked at. So, on the hypothesis that subjects *can* tell when they are being looked at, they must also be able to tell the difference between being looked and having their twin looked at; but in this case, we would seem to be back to a situation where there is no possible physical explanation for such a detection, since there is no physical difference between these two conditions. Since Sheldrake's explanation is a physical one, it would seem to be unable to explain this type of situation.

On the other hand, if we simply rule out the validity of the studies in which people can detect being seen on TV monitors, then it is much easier to explain the more proximate detection abilities of subjects in terms of subliminal awareness of the presence of another living being by means of slight changes in atmospheric and other environmental conditions, of the kind that Gendlin discusses. And in that case, it is not necessary to descend to the quantum level for an explanation.

References

Fodor, J. (1975),*The Language of Thought* (Cambridge, MA: Harvard University Press).

Fodor, J. (1987), *Psychosemantics* (Cambridge, MA: MIT Press).

Gendlin, E. (1992), 'The primacy of the body, not the primacy of perception', *Man and World,* **25**, pp. 341–53.

Husserl, E. (1900/1913), *Logical Investigations*, trans. J.N. Findlay (New York: Humanities Press).

Husserl, E. (1913/1931), *Ideas*, trans. W.R. Boyce Gibson (London: Collier 1931; from *Ideen zu einer reinen Phänomenologie und phänomenologischen Philosophie,* 1913).

Husserl, E. (1962), *Phänomenologische Psychologie* (Den Haag: Martinus Nijhoff, original German ed. 1900).

Merleau-Ponty, M. (1942/1963), *The Structure of Behavior,* trans. A. Fischer (Boston, MA: Beacon; original French edition 1942).

Newton, N. (1996), *Foundations of Understanding* (Amsterdam: John Benjamins).

Newton, N. (2000), 'Representation in theories of embodied cognition', *Behavioral and Brain Sciences,* **24** (1), pp. 89–90.

Newton, N. (2001), 'Emergence and the uniqueness of consciousness', *Journal of Consciousness Studies,* **8** (9–10), pp. 47–59.

Newton, N. (2003), 'Representation in theories of embodied cognition', in *Embodiment in Phenomenology and Cognitive Science*, ed. Shaun Gallagher and Natalie Depraz, Special Issue of *Theoria et Historia Scientiarum: International Journal for Interdisciplinary Studies,* Spring 2003, pp. 181–94.

Newton, N. (2004), 'The art of representation: Support for an enactive approach', *Behavioral and Brain Sciences,* **27** (3), p. 411.

Thelen, E., Schoner, G., and Scheier, C. (2001), 'The dynamics of embodiment: A field theory of infant perseverative reaching', *Behavioral and Brain Sciences,* **24**, pp. 1–86.

Thomas, Nigel (1989), 'Experience and theory as determinants of attitudes toward mental representation', *American Journal of Psychology,* **102**, pp. 395–412.

DAVID FONTANA

Rupert Sheldrake and the Staring Effect

I: The Reality of the Staring Effect

In the absence of sensory clues, can we really be aware that someone is staring at us? The evidence, as reviewed by Rupert Sheldrake, suggests quite strongly that we can, yet many refuse to accept this evidence despite the fact that other human abilities have sometimes been acknowledged on the strength of rather less support. The problem that prevents the general acceptance of the staring effect is the absence of any known mechanism to explain how, without suitable sensory input, it can possibly occur. The absence of such a mechanism means that if we accept that it does happen we have necessarily to recognise the limitations of our known laws of science, and this we are reluctant to do. These laws stand us in good stead elsewhere and prompt many to insist that the existence of phenomena that contradicts them must be demonstrated to the satisfaction of even the sternest critic on the basis that exceptional claims require exceptional levels of proof. In spite of the fact that the staring effect has been demonstrated significantly in a number of well-controlled experiments, failure consistently to replicate these results is therefore readily accepted as convincing evidence that the former are flawed in some way, and that the staring effect is not to be taken seriously.

However, strict adherence to the need for consistent replication can have certain disadvantages in the context of human psychology. By their very nature, some human abilities tend to be fleeting and elusive, and if we demand they be demonstrated repeatedly — and to order — at the same evidential level expected from investigations in other areas of science we risk handicapping ourselves in our attempt to study them more deeply. It is notoriously difficult to replicate exactly the results of many psychological experiments due to the wide range of variables that influence human performance, particularly where different samples of individuals are being investigated or the same samples are re-tested under different circumstances. Thus the occasional failure in replication is normally not taken as an indication that the ability under scrutiny is illusory, but as an indication that we need to study the part played by these variables in inhibiting performance. In the case of the staring effect, unless we decide *a priori* that it cannot happen in the absence of a known explanatory mechanism, it seems clear that the positive results now yielded by a number of studies are sufficiently impressive for us to adopt as a working hypothesis the proposition that the effect and the ability responsible for it may be real. A working hypothesis is based upon the recognition that a particular body of evidence, however much it may go against existing models of reality, is strong enough to warrant further research and to allow discussion as to the implications it may have for the rest of human knowledge. Demonstration, in the context of the working hypothesis, is thus seen as acceptable evidentially even in the absence of explanation.

In addition to the experimental evidence that serves to support the hypothesis that the staring effect may be real, Rupert Sheldrake refers to findings suggesting that belief in this effect is accepted not only by the great majority of children but by the great majority of adults. The studies concerned indicate that more than 80 per cent of women and more than 70 per cent of men believe not only that they know when others are staring at them, but that they can stare at others and make them turn around. Unless we are to consign without obvious reason some 80 per cent of our fellow men and women to the limbo of the irredeemably superstitious, we are bound as psychologists to take these findings seriously and enquire *why* people maintain this conviction. Do they do so simply in response to the beliefs of others, or are they speaking from personal experience? The latter would seem the more likely explanation. After all, the staring effect is something that each of us can readily put to the test. True we may be deceived about our personal experience — for example we may remember only the occasions when staring seems to work and conveniently forget all the many occasions when it does not — but it is equally true that we may be deceiving ourselves if we fail to credit our fellows with the ability to judge personal experience with at least some degree of accuracy.

In the case of the staring effect, this experience may be based not just upon quantity but upon quality, that is not just upon the frequency with which someone senses they are being stared at but upon the emotional reaction they experience when it happens. Similarly the starer may be aware, from physical clues, that the person at whom they are staring also appears to exhibit an emotional reaction of some sort. I may perhaps be permitted to offer a personal example of the latter experience, since it was one of the first occasions in my adult life when I became aware that the staring effect might be real. The person at whom I was (inadvertently) staring looked over her shoulder at me the moment she came into view with an expression of such startled surprise that I was equally taken aback when our eyes met. Even had I known and called out her name, her reaction could not have been more marked. At the time I was staring out of my study window at the empty road that runs virtually parallel to the left of my house (which is on a corner), and she came into view walking away from me. Unless she had eyes in the back of her head there were no sensory clues that would have betrayed my presence to her. The window at which I was seated was closed at the time, I was sitting still, and she would have had no reason to suppose I was there or any reason to wish to see me. The road is an exceptionally quiet one, and there were no distractions in the vicinity of my house that might have caught her attention. Anecdotal evidence such as this only carries conviction for the person who experiences it, but it can at times suggest ideas for further research. Thus it would be useful to establish if emotional reactions similar to the one witnessed by me on this occasion are common in the context of the staring effect. If they are, this may help explain why such an overwhelming number of adults believe in the reality of the effect — perhaps they know the emotional charge sometimes involved. Investigations into the differing nature of this charge from person to person might also help advance our knowledge of what is taking place and perhaps why it happens.

II: The Implications of the Staring Effect

It can hardly be doubted that the implications of the staring effect, if genuine, for our understanding of consciousness and of the mind–brain relationship are, to put it mildly, far-reaching. One of the most important of these implications has to do with the location (or non-localisation) of consciousness. Max Velmans in particular has long argued that consciousness extends throughout the body rather than being localised within the head or any other part of it. One of the examples he gives is that when we prick our finger the pain is felt in the finger and not in the head (Velmans, 2000). Further support for this argument comes from an exercise in the training of meditators that involves moving consciousness around the body in order to dispel the common misconception that it is located some-where behind the eyes. This is an experiment that anyone can try, and involves placing the awareness exclusively in the sense of touch — first in the feeling of the feet against the floor, then in the ankles as they are gently flexed, and so on upwards through the legs and the body, the arms and the neck, and finally the head and the scalp. The object of the exercise is to allow the meditator to experience for him or herself the fluid nature of consciousness, and to recognise that the reason we habitually suppose it to be in the head is simply because five of the six senses are exclusively located there.

However, in spite of its fluid nature, consciousness in this meditation exercise (and in the pricked finger) remains linked to the body's sensory — and therefore physical — mechanisms. The finding that it is not solely in the head complicates the process of establishing the true nature of consciousness, but a major speculative leap is required before we can suggest with any conviction that consciousness extends *beyond* the physical body and can embrace not only physical realities outside the unaided reach of normal sense perception but perhaps even non-physical realities such as the thoughts and emotions of others. Yet until the advent of scientific materialism in the eighteenth and nineteenth centuries this suggestion was accepted as a matter of course by most people in the West — and still is accepted by countless millions of our fellow beings elsewhere in the world. It is easy to dismiss such a belief as superstition, a pre-scientific effort to find meaning in a largely mysterious universe, but an alternative possibility is that for some people at least this belief was based upon direct experience.

Rupert Sheldrake takes up this point in his argument that consciousness is in fact a field phenomenon. The most striking feature of this argument is concerned with the third aspect of the mind–brain problem to which he refers, namely that the subject who perceives and the object of perception (i.e. the observer and the observed) are linked together into a single system. In his view the perceptual field of the observer extends 'out beyond the brain to include or enclose the object of perception'. In the case of the staring effect, the perceptual field of the person responsible for the staring interacts with the perceptual field of the person at whom he or she is staring. At a stroke consciousness is thus presented not as a function solely (or even perhaps primarily) of brain activity, but as a thing in itself, obeying its own laws and not subject to normal physical constraints.

Amongst the various possible ways in which we might conceptualise this, the model proposed by Chris Clarke (1996) is perhaps the most appealing, namely that conscious perception depends essentially upon quantum entanglement between the quantum states of the observer and the quantum states of what is observed. Quantum entanglement, which refers to the propensity of each member of a pair of particles emitted from a common source to evidence correlations between their behaviour even when separated from each other by relatively large distances, is only partially understood (if indeed such phenomena can ever be 'understood' in our usual meaning of the term), but Rupert Sheldrake's implication, following on from Radin (2004), is that as we develop more complex explanatory models of how entanglement takes place, the idea that mind (or consciousness) fields exist that are entangled with the rest of the universe may come to look increasingly plausible. If such is the case, the staring effect may be accommodated without undue difficulty.

Should the idea of entangled, interpenetrating mind fields prove increasingly to fit the models generated by quantum physics (and we have to be cautious and stress the *if*), then much of the distinction between subject and object will disappear. There are intriguing parallels between this possibility and the *yogachara* teachings of Mahayana Buddhism that originated in the fourth century CE. In terms of these teachings, things exist only as processes of knowledge. Thus there are no separate objects and no separate subjects, simply a flow of perceptions that produce the appearance of external objects within the mind (or rather within the mind field), together with the delusion of an individual self that is separate from these perceptions. As with the model of quantum entanglement, the staring effect would seem readily accommodated within these teachings. All mind fields are simply aspects of one interpenetrating field of perceptual experience, and the teachings insist that through intensive meditation practice one can become conscious of this fact and incidentally develop a heightened awareness of mind fields other than one's own.

If the staring effect is real, this opens the way to a whole raft of questions about how the entanglement of mind fields is likely to work. For example, to what exactly is the recipient reacting? Do the physical actions of the starer as he turns his head and directs his attention register on this field, or does the field register only mental events? If the latter, what mental events are involved? The starer's motivation to stare? The thoughts going through his head as he reacts to the person at whom he is staring? The emotions he or she arouses in him? Or is it a combination of all these things? Perhaps the answer to these questions may help us understand why it is that on many (probably the majority) of occasions we are *not* aware when someone is staring at us. Do some of us respond only if there is some perceived threat in the stare? Do some of us respond only if the stare is one of admiration or only if it is one of disapproval? Do some of us respond only if there is a measure of compatibility between our mind field and that of the starer? Are we always aware at an unconscious level of being stared at, but only aware consciously if we have a special sensitivity? Is there perhaps some form of mental filtering mechanism at work that prevents us from being invaded by the stares and thoughts of others? Further research, taking in self-reports and autonomic reactions, might help answer some of these questions

III: Conclusion

Whichever way we look at it, the staring effect is not one we can ignore. We should not be dissuaded from further research by *a priori* convictions that the effect cannot happen. It might be too much to hope that research into it is ever likely to attract large grants. Research institutions (or rather those responsible for decision-making within them) are far too cautious for that. But if large-scale studies could be mounted there should be little difficulty in establishing once and for all whether the effect is genuine or not. And if it is genuine, we can then move on to investigate what light it throws upon our understanding of our own nature.

References

Clarke, C.J.S. (1996), *Reality Through the Looking Glass: Science and Awareness in the Postmodern World* (Edinburgh: Floris Books).

Radin, D. (2004), 'The feeling of being stared at: An analysis and replication', *Journal of the Society for Psychical Research*, **68**, pp. 245–52.

Velmans, M. (2000), *Understanding Consciousness* (London and Philadelphia: Routledge).

CHRISTOPHER C. FRENCH

A Closer Look at Sheldrake's Treatment of Rattee's Data

I will limit my comments on Rupert Sheldrake's articles to two points, one specific and one general, both relating to his first article in which he reviews the available empirical literature on the alleged sense of being stared at.

The specific point relates to the brief description provided by Sheldrake of an experiment carried out by Neal Rattee in 1996 under my supervision. As Sheldrake points out, Rattee's results would have just reached statistical significance if a one-tailed test had been employed instead of a two-tailed test. Two questions that Sheldrake does not address are (a) whether or not a one-tailed test is appropriate in this case and (b) if it is, what is the direction of the predicted difference in skin conductance levels between the stare and non-stare trials?

Every first-year psychology student is taught that it is appropriate to use a two-tailed statistical test when one is predicting a difference between two groups or conditions without predicting the direction of the difference and a one-tailed test if one is predicting the direction of the difference. In practice, most experimental psychologists prefer to avoid using one-tailed tests at all. One-tailed tests are less conservative in that one is twice as likely to obtain a statistically significant result if one applies a one-tailed test instead of a two-tailed test to a particular set of data provided that the difference between the two means is in the 'predicted' direction. One problem with the use of one-tailed tests (and the reason for the scare quotes around 'predicted' in the last sentence) is that it is sometimes possible to think up a superficially plausible reason for why one might have 'predicted' a difference in a particular direction *after* one has carried out an analysis and discovered that one has obtained a result which is only statistically significant if a one-tailed test is used. The suspicion might then arise that, had the difference in means been in the opposite direction, one could have produced an equally plausible reason for 'predicting' a difference in *that* direction. Such circumstances arise particularly for complex experimental designs involving lots of interacting factors, but also in situations where previous research has produced conflicting results. If one can find reasons to favour experiments producing outcomes in one particular direction as being methodologically superior to those finding the opposite pattern, one could again attempt to justify the use of a one-tailed hypothesis. It is precisely because most experimentalists are sophisticated enough to appreciate the ease with which such *post hoc* justifications can sometimes be conjured up that they mostly prefer to avoid the use of one-tailed tests altogether — unless, of course, their data absolutely forces them to make use of them! Experimental psychologists are only human after all, despite claims to the contrary.

Having said all that, there are also situations where the predicted direction of the difference between two means is so obvious on the basis of theoretical and previous experimental results that the use of a one-tailed test would hardly raise an eyebrow. So what was the situation with respect to Neal Rattee's final year undergraduate project? Some commentators may feel that a two-tailed test was the more appropriate option simply because previous research had apparently shown different patterns of electrodermal reactivity in response to staring depending upon the nature of the participants being stared at (e.g., Braud *et al.*, 1993; see below for details). But is it the case that closer examination of the theoretical justification and previous experimental results would show that Sheldrake was justified in recommending the use of a one-tailed test on Rattee's data?

Sheldrake is curiously vague with respect to why measuring galvanic skin response (GSR) would be an appropriate technique to use in order to investigate the alleged ability to detect unseen gaze, limiting himself to stating that tests had been done in which GSR was recorded automatically 'as in lie-detector tests'. It goes without saying that readers of the *Journal of Consciousness Studies* would know that the basic principle underlying the use of (so-called) lie-detector tests is that most people become more aroused when telling a lie. This leads to activation of the sympathetic nervous system and that leads to increased sweating. Sweating causes the conductivity of the skin to increase (or, to put it another way, the resistance to decrease) and this is what the GSR is measuring. Although not explicitly stated by Sheldrake, readers would implicitly assume that, if some of us can indeed sense when we are being stared at, this would result in higher levels of skin conductance for stare trials compared to non-stare trials on the assumption that being stared at would make us feel uncomfortable and therefore more aroused. It is clear from Sheldrake's description of Robert Baker's demonstration that he is implying that people typically do indeed feel uncomfortable when they sense that they are being stared at. So, is this what previous studies using GSR have actually demonstrated?

The answer is 'not always'. It depends upon the nature of the person being stared at, the so-called 'staree'. For example, in Braud et al.'s (1993) study, untrained starees showed increased arousal on stare trials compared to non-stare trials, as one might expect. Participants who had undergone 'connectedness training', however, showed the opposite pattern of results, i.e., they were less aroused for staring trials than for non-staring trials. This training involved 'intellectual and experiential exercises involving feelings of interconnectedness with other people' (p. 381). On the basis of previous experiments such as this, would it have been more appropriate to use a one-tailed test in analysing Rattee's data?

If we are to do so, we must specify the direction of the predicted difference in means between staring and non-staring trials for the dependent variable employed, i.e., skin conductance. Rattee's participants were 27 first-year psychology students participating 'as a course requirement' and three final year undergraduates. They did not receive any special training. Therefore, one could only reasonably predict that their arousal levels (and skin conductance) would be higher on stare trials compared to non-stare trials (or else use a non-directional two-tailed test). As stated in the experimental report, 'A detect score was calculated for each subject by subtracting total SCL [skin conductance levels] during non-stare periods from that during the stare periods on the basis that the mean chance expectation would be 0.' The actual difference in SCL was '–21.64' (S.D. = '68.97'). Although the actual units of measurement are not specified, it is clear that the (untrained) participants were slightly *more* aroused during the non-stare trials than the stare trials. Thus, if we had used a one-tailed test predicting that they would have been less aroused for such trials, we would again have had to accept the null hypothesis. Whichever way you look at it, Rattee's data cannot be said to support the hypothesis that people are able to detect unseen gaze even at the non-conscious level of autonomic activity.

The second, more general, point I would like to make is one that is likely to have occurred to many readers of *JCS*. In discussing possible artefacts that might explain the 'repeatable positive results' in studies of the detection of unseen gaze, Sheldrake takes each in turn (e.g., sensory leakage, cheating, implicit learning) and attempts to dismiss each of them by pointing out that there are studies which have controlled for each effect and have still produced positive results. However, without a reasonable number of studies that produce positive results while controlling for *all* of these potential artefacts simultaneously, it is not possible to rule them out as possible causes of positive findings. A recent meta-analysis of remote staring studies by Schmidt et al. (2004) concluded that 'there are hints of an effect, but also a shortage of independent replications and theoretical concepts' (p. 235). More pertinent to the current discussion is their comment that 'one has to be careful when interpreting the remote staring data because there is a lack of high-quality studies and such studies may reduce the overall effect size or even show that the effect does not exist' (p. 245). Unless and until such studies have been carried out and reported, no definitive conclusions can be reasonably be drawn regarding the reality or otherwise of the alleged sense of being stared at. The positive results reported to date, however, provide a very strong justification for further and better quality investigations of this intriguing topic in the future.

References

Braud, W., Shafer, D. & Andrews, S. (1993), 'Reactions to an unseen gaze (remote attention): A review, with new data on autonomic staring detection', *Journal of Parapsychology*, **57**, pp. 373–90.
Schmidt, S., Schneider, R., Utts, J. & Walach, H. (2004), 'Distant intentionality and the feeling of being stared at: Two meta-analyses', *British Journal of Psychology*, **95**, pp. 235–47.

DEAN RADIN

The Sense of Being Stared At: A Preliminary Meta-Analysis

Abstract: Meta-analysis of 60 experiments investigating the conscious sense of being stared at suggests that the reported effects may reflect a genuine ability. A subset of 10 of these studies, designed to preclude implicit learning of sensory cues, resulted in a homogeneous distribution of effect sizes and a weighted mean effect size substantially beyond chance expectation ($p = 5 \times 10^{-17}$).

Two types of experiments have been conducted to investigate the commonly reported 'sense of being stared at' — those based on conscious reports and those based on unconscious physiological responses. The first class, described by Sheldrake in this issue, studies the ability of a 'staree' to consciously detect being stared at, typically by a 'starer' located behind the staree. This paper reports a preliminary meta-analytic examination of these experiments.

The second class of experiments, reported by Schlitz and Braud (1997) and others, investigates whether a starer's gaze over a closed-circuit video link, under conditions that rigorously exclude sensory cues, can be detected as unconscious fluctuations in a staree's skin conductance (Braud & Schlitz, 1989; 1991). Schmidt *et al.* (2004) report a meta-analysis of 15 such experiments involving a total of 379 individual testing sessions. That analysis provided significant evidence for a distant staring effect, a homogeneous distribution of effect sizes, and no evidence of a selective reporting problem. Those studies suggest that an unconscious sense of being stared at is a genuine, independently repeatable effect, providing proof-of-principle for the effects reported by Sheldrake.

Method

I excluded from consideration a large-scale staring study conducted at the NEMO Science Centre in Amsterdam and also web-based staring studies, as trials collected in those studies were unsupervised (Sheldrake, this issue). From Sheldrake (1998; 1999; 2000a,b; 2003), and citations therein (e.g., Coover, 1913; Colwell *et al.*, 2000; Lobach & Bierman, 2004; Poortman, 1959; Radin, 2004), I identified 60 relevant experiments reporting a total of 33,357 trials collected under one or more investigator's supervision. These studies involved three categories of control for implicit learning of sensory cues: tests conducted in close proximity with trial-by-trial feedback, tests conducted in close proximity without feedback, and tests conducted by looking through windows and without feedback. Of the 60 studies, the majority (88%) fell in the first and third categories.

The raw data in each study was the number of times the staree successfully identified being stared at or not stared at (each success called a *hit*), and the total number of trials conducted in the study (N). Hits and trials were used to form a per study 'hit rate' as $p_1 = hits/N$, and then p_1 was used to form a standard normal variable $z = (p_1-p_0)/se$, where $p_0 = 0.5$ (meaning an equal *a priori* likelihood of being in a staring or non-staring condition), $se = \sqrt{p_0 q_0 / N}$ and $q_0 = 1-p_0$. Effect size per trial (per study) was determined as $e = z / \sqrt{N}$, and a weighted mean effect size assuming a fixed effects model (FEM) was formed with a weighting factor based on the inverse of the squared standard error, $w = 1/se^2$, which in this case is equivalent to $w = 4N$ (Hedges, 1994). Then a weighted mean effect size was formed as $\bar{e} = \sum (w \times e) / \sum w$, where the sums are taken over N studies. To assess the homogeneity of effect sizes, the statistic Q was determined, where $Q = \sum (w \times e^2) - \left[\sum (w \times e)\right]^2 / \sum w$ with $N-1$ degrees of freedom. Q follows the chi-squared distribution.

Results

Figure 1 shows the cumulative mean hit rate across the 60 studies, with one standard error bars. It is clear that the mean hit rate stabilizes to just over 54%, where 50% is expected by chance. The FEM weighted mean effect size was significantly above chance, $\bar{e} = 0.089 \pm 0.003$ (mean ± standard error), $z = 32.5$, $p = 10^{-232}$, and the distribution of effects was significantly heterogeneous, $Q = 763.3$ (58 df), $p = 10^{-123}$. Because of the heterogeneity, a more conservative random effects model was also determined (REM, Hedges & Vevea, 1998). The

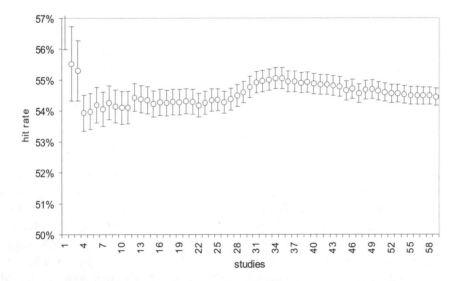

Figure 1. Cumulative mean hit rate for 60 sense-of-being-stared-at experiments, with one standard error bars.

REM weighted mean effect size remained significantly above chance, $\bar{e} = 0.114 \pm 0.010$, $z = 10.9$, $p = 10^{-28}$, and the distribution of effects also remained heterogeneous, $Q = 167.8$ (58 df), $p = 10^{-12}$.

Discussion

One possible explanation for the heterogeneity is a selective reporting bias. A common way to visualize whether selective reporting might be a problem is with a 'funnel plot' graphing effect size vs. sample size. If such a plot is positively skewed, it indicates that small sample-size studies with negative outcomes were probably not reported. Use of a technique known as 'trim and fill' can be applied to this plot to algorithmically identify and fill in the potentially missing studies to make the plot symmetric (Duval & Tweedie, 2000). A new weighted mean effect size can then be formed using the missing studies to form a conservative estimate of the 'true' effect size.

The black circles and white diamond in the funnel plot in Figure 2 show the effect size for each of the 60 reported studies. The positive skew in this plot indicates that this database probably has a selective reporting problem. The trim and fill algorithm identified that six studies were required to make the plot symmetric; these are shown as the white circles in Figure 2. The dashed vertical line indicates the FEM weighted mean effect size. Recalculating both the FEM and REM means effects after adding the six estimated studies resulted in slightly smaller but still highly significant mean effect sizes: $\bar{e}$ (FEM) $= 0.078 \pm 0.003$, $z = 28.9$, $p = 10^{-184}$ and $\bar{e}$ (REM) $= 0.072 \pm 0.010$, $z = 7.15$, $p = 10^{-13}$.

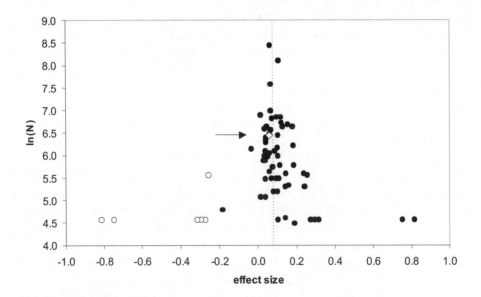

Figure 2. Funnel plot for 59 sense-of-being-stared-at experiments (black dots) and six studies identified by the 'trim and fill' algorithm (white dots). The arrow pointing to the white diamond indicates the effect size measured in a recent replication attempt using a computer-based, automated recording system (Radin, 2004).

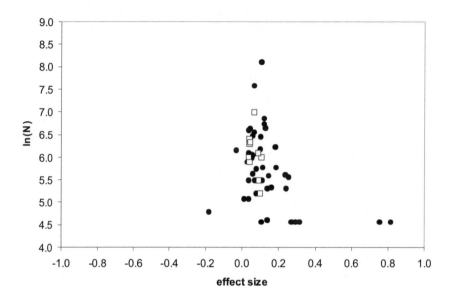

Figure 3. Funnel plot comparing 42 experiments conducted in close proximity and with trial by trial feedback (black circles), and 10 experiments conducted at a distance, looking through a window, and without feedback (white squares).

By eliminating 19 studies with the largest Q values, the effect size heterogeneity becomes homogeneous. All of the eliminated studies involved close proximity designs with trial-by-trial feedback. With the remaining homogeneously distributed studies, the FEM and REM mean weighted effect sizes remain significant; the more conservative e (REM) = 0.063 ± 0.007, $p = 10^{-19}$.

To examine the possibility that studies with especially large outcomes might have been due to poorer controls for sensory cues, two funnel plots were formed, as shown in Figure 3. The black circles in this figure show 42 studies involving designs with close proximity and trial-by-trial feedback, and the white squares show 10 studies conducted through windows without feedback. It is evident that both the heterogeneity and the selective reporting problem are due to the close-proximity studies. The 10 better-controlled studies are homogenously distributed and do not show evidence of selective reporting. The FEM weighted mean effect size for the through-the-window studies (which is the appropriate effect size model given the homogeneity of effect sizes) is highly significant ($p = 4.8 \times 10^{-17}$). Comparison of the FEM and REM models is shown in Table 1.

Comparison of the close-proximity vs. the through-the-window studies shows that the latter had significantly lower mean effect sizes in both fixed and random effects models ($z = -4.96$, $p = 10^{-6}$, two-tailed; $z = -2.00$, $p = 0.05$, two-tailed, respectively). This suggests that the mean effect size for close-proximity studies might be inflated due to implicit learning of subliminal cues, but that explanation is confounded by the likelihood of selective reporting, as shown by the funnel plot and suggested by the heterogeneity of this class of experiments.

Model	Through window		Close proximity	
	FEM	REM	FEM	REM
e	0.060	0.064	0.100	0.131
se	0.007	0.030	0.004	0.015
z	8.31	2.14	27.84	8.78
p	4.8×10^{-17}	0.016	6.4×10^{-171}	8.3×10^{-19}
Q	10.74	0.80	648.75	115.40
df	9	9	41	41
p	0.29	0.99	2.4×10^{-110}	5.3×10^{-9}

Table 1. Comparison of fixed and random effects models for sense of being stared at studies conducted with higher controls for implicit learning of sensory cues (staring through windows without feedback) and lower controls (staring at close proximity with feedback).

One way to assess the impact of the selective reporting on the overall evidence is to estimate how many missing studies are required to nullify the overall effect. Two models of estimating this missing 'filedrawer' were employed. The first, proposed by Rosenthal (1979; 1991), asks how many studies averaging an overall null effect would be required to reduce the overall level of significance to just above the conventional level of statistical significance, i.e. $p > 0.05$. The second, proposed by Scargle (2000) and independently by Hsu (2002), asks the same question but assumes that the missing studies would average to a slightly negative effect rather than to a null effect. The Scargle/Hsu assumption is based on the expectation that all studies with positive outcomes at $p < 0.05$ (one-tailed) *or* with negative outcomes at $p < 0.05$ (two-tailed) are published. The asymmetry in thresholds for assigning statistical 'significance' to positive and negative outcomes provides a more conservative filedrawer estimate.

Table 2 shows that the estimated filedrawer contains between 1,417 and 7,729 missing studies, depending on which model one wishes to adopt. Converting these figures into an estimated number of missing individual trials, based on the average number of trials per reported study ($N = 565$), results in the range of 800,000 to 3 million missing trials. These figures seem implausible given the relatively small numbers of investigators who have demonstrated interest in this line of experimentation.

Method	Filedrawer estimate	Trials
Rosenthal	7,729	3,045,210
Scargle/Hsu	1,417	800,885

Table 2. Filedrawer estimates using Rosenthal and Scargle/Hsu methods.

As more of these studies are conducted, new meta-analyses will undoubtedly assess in finer detail design elements such as the types of controls employed, how conditions were randomized, how the tests were supervised, how data were recorded, and so on. Examination of such moderator variables will help explain the overall heterogeneity. Based on Schmidt *et al.*'s (2004) meta-analysis of similar experiments involving rigorous controls against sensory cues, it seems likely that future meta-analyses will continue to show that some proportion of these effects reflect a genuine but poorly understood 'sense'.

References

Braud, W. and Schlitz, M. (1989), 'Possible role of intuitive data sorting in electrodermal biological psychokinesis (bio-PK)', *Journal of the American Society for Psychical Research*, **83** (4), pp. 289–302.

Braud, W. and Schlitz, M. (1991), 'Consciousness interactions with remote biological systems: anomalous intentionality effects', *Subtle Energies and Energy Medicine*, **2**, pp. 1–46.

Colwell, J., Schröder, S. & Sladen, D. (2000), 'The ability to detect unseen staring: A literature review and empirical tests', *British Journal of Psychology*, **91**, pp. 71–85.

Coover, J.E. (1913), 'The feeling of being stared at – experimental', *American Journal of Psychology*, **24**, pp. 570–5.

Duval, S. & Tweedie, R. (2000), 'A nonparametric "trim and fill" method of accounting for publication bias in meta-analysis', *Journal of the American Statistical Association*, **95**, pp. 89–98.

Hedges, L.V. (1994), 'Fixed effect models', in *The Handbook of Research Synthesis*, ed. L.V. Hedges & H. Cooper (New York: Russell Sage Foundation).

Hedges, L.V., & Vevea, J.L. (1998), 'Fixed- and random-effects models in meta-analysis', *Psychological Methods*, **3**, pp. 486–504.

Hsu, L.M. (2002), 'Fail-safe Ns for one- versus two-tailed tests lead to different conclusions about publication bias', *Understanding Statistics*, **1** (2), p. 85–100.

Lobach, E. & Bierman, D.J. (2004), 'The invisible gaze: Three attempts to replicate Sheldrake's staring effects', *Proceedings of the Parapsychological Association Annual Convention*, 2004.

Poortman, J.J. (1959), 'The feeling of being stared at', *Journal of the Society for Psychical Research*, **40**, pp. 4–12.

Radin, D.I. (2004), 'On the sense of being stared at: An analysis and pilot replication', *Journal of the Society for Psychical Research*, **68**, pp. 246–53.

Rosenthal, R. (1979), 'The "file drawer problem" and tolerance for null results, *Psychological Bulletin*, **86**, pp. 638–41.

Rosenthal, R. (1991), *Meta-Analytic Procedures for Social Research*, Rev. ed. (Newbury Park, CA: Sage).

Scargle, J.D. (2000), 'Publication bias: The "file-drawer problem" in scientific inference', *Journal of Scientific Exploration*, **14** (1), pp. 91–106.

Schlitz, M. and Braud, W. (1997), 'Distant intentionality and healing: Assessing the evidence', *Journal of Alternative Therapies*, **3** (6), pp. 62–73.

Schmidt, S., Schneider, R., Utts, J. & Walach, H. (2004), 'Distant intentionality and the feeling of being stared at: Two meta-analyses', *British Journal of Psychology*, **95**, pp. 235–47.

Sheldrake, R. (1998), 'The sense of being stared at: Experiments in schools', *Journal of the Society of Psychical Research*, **62**, pp. 311–23.

Sheldrake, R. (1999), 'The "sense of being stared at" confirmed by simple experiments', *Biology Forum*, **92**, pp. 53–76.

Sheldrake, R. (2000a), 'The "sense of being stared at" does not depend on known sensory clues', *Biology Forum*, **93**, pp. 209–24.

Sheldrake, R. (2000b), 'The sense of being stared at: Effects of blindfolding subjects and giving them feedback', *Journal of the Society of Psychical Research*.

Sheldrake, R. (2003), *The Sense of Being Stared At* (New York: Crown Publishers).

MARILYN SCHLITZ

The Discourse of Controversial Science:
The Sceptic–Proponent Debate on Remote Staring

Science is a dominant paradigm in Western thought and action. As members of modern society we frequently turn our trust to the experience and purported knowledge of scientists to shape our understanding of the world around us. In this epistemological capacity, scientists are understood to be objective truth-seekers guided by pre-established methods and procedures for demarcating that which is true from that which is false. In a public sphere free from domination, such as that proposed by social philosopher Jurgen Habermas, in his now classic works (1979; 1981), communication should move toward understanding among members of differing but equal social segments. Research in the sociology and anthropology of science, however, reveals the subjective and often arbitrary nature of scientific practice. Scientists are involved in a form of cultural exchange in which preexisting assumptions, belief systems, social relations, and power positionings guide their views of reality. From this vantage point, science with a capital S is better expressed by a relativist set of small s's that correspond to differing social positions and subcultures. What is truth to one group may be false to another, and vice versa, although some views clearly dominate over others. Social norms influence the knowledge constitutive interests of science (Habermas, 1971) — shaping what is or is not acceptable as reasonable research. All understanding is constrained by borders which structure the communication genre (Bahktin, 1986). Discourses about scientific truth are shaped and reshaped as epistemology and politics become one.

Debates over controversial areas of science are especially useful for deconstructing the ideological nature of truth in Western society. Disputes over the legitimacy of specific research topics, such as the studies of remote staring by Rupert Sheldrake, debated in this special issue of the *Journal of Consciousness Studies*, provide a useful testing ground for mapping social assumptions about science and the interplay of power and language in scientific discourse. As we consider this specific area of research, we can see Dr. Sheldrake's work and the ensuing critique within the context of the sceptic–proponent debate in parapsychology. One way to understand this debate is within a communication model that posits ideal speech situations and an open exchange between equals (Habermas, 1971;1979). How and why does communication fail in the context of truth construction in scientific discourse? These are questions we must ask as we complete our reading of the various positions articulated in this volume.

Parapsychology is a fledgling discipline committed to the scientific study of *psi* phenomena, including extrasensory perception (ESP) and psychokinesis (PK). While parapsychology researchers have adopted scientific methods, standards, and language, the research occupies a marginalized position relative to the scientific establishment (McClenon, 1984; Mauskopf and McVaugh, 1980). It represents a heterodox discipline in comparison to the scientific orthodoxy (Hess, 1993). A discourse has been constructed over the past century in which scientists have debated the pros and cons of parapsychology research as a legitimate domain of scientific inquiry (e.g., Jastrow, 1900; Hansel, 1980; Honorton, 1985; Hyman, 1985; Alcock *et al.*, 2002).

Proponents and sceptics alike draw on common forms and rhetorical styles to argue the case for and against the existence of psychic phenomena. Nowhere is this more clear than in this special issue, which provides a forum for the debate over the nature and potential reach of consciousness. This forum provides evidence of a shared scientific speech community. At the same time, however, the juxtaposition of opposing sides within the debate reveals fundamental tensions within society — suggestive of what C.P. Snow (1959) referred to as 'two cultures'. Embedded within the parapsychology debate are oppositional relations and social alignments that have emerged in the struggle to control what is acceptable or unacceptable as legitimate science or valid knowledge. Lines have been drawn between the proponents, who argue that there is evidence to support remote staring, and sceptics, who argue that the purported results are due to artifacts, wishful thinking, or outright fraud on the part of the experimenters. Both proponents and sceptics compete to be the scientific voice of reason when dealing with claims of the paranormal. In constructing a self/other opposition, the two sides portray one another as different as well as morally wrong (Hess, 1993).

The discussion of a common forum, such as we find in this journal, implies an orientation toward reaching understanding among those engaged in the discourse on consciousness and the role that psi phenomena may or may not play. Again following Habermas, we may examine the role of language in the development of consensus between opposing sides within the debate. Habermas (1981, p. 101) states that communicative rationality involves the 'unifying consensus-building force of argumentative speech, in which different participants overcome their merely subjective views and, owing to the mutuality of rationally motivated conviction, assure themselves of both the unity of the objective world and the intersubjectivity of their lifeworld'. As we look at the nature of this special issue, we see that perhaps reciprocity in communication provides a consensual standard for the resolution of conflict. Or does it?

The formal parapsychology debate, of which Sheldrake's remote staring research is part, centres on issues of methodology, experimental controls, data analysis, and theory construction. It is at the levels of interpretation and reciprocity related to these issues that aspirations and realities of communication break down. This can be seen in the excerpts from members of the sceptical community, cited by Sheldrake in his lead essay, who have dismissed the data. Ideology and on-going power relations represent serious challenges to the ideal speech situation (White, 1988). Guidelines in scientific practice are frequently vague. Still, there are assumptions about what falls within the boundaries of truth.

At the level of the scientific academy, there are efforts to maintain boundaries between what is acceptable or unacceptable within the confines of scientific practice (Gieryn, 1983). Access to scientific forums requires conformance to standards set by the orthodoxy, which exclude psi phenomena from the realm of possibilities. The opportunity to publish in accepted journals, to participate in selected conferences, and to join professional societies are the product of on-going social relations based on existing power relations. That this debate is happening in the pages of this journal speaks to the vibrancy that comes when voices of difference reveal the sociological nature of truth construction. In most academic journals, however, those who fail to pass the accepted criteria, even in the face of work that is based on preestablished standards, are frequently excluded from the process of open and effective communication (see McClenon, 1984). Validity claims, so central to Habermas' agenda, change in the face of new information — often reinforcing preexisting assumptions and power relations. Fairness, impartiality, and equal distribution of opportunities are often lost in the course of scientific practice.

Even in the face of collaborative speech events, such as we find in a meta-critique of this special issue, the democratization of communication frequently fails. It is clear, especially in areas of controversy such as parapsychology, that speakers do not always reach agreement. A failure to communicate is based on assumptions that precede specific speech events. While Habermas (1979) argues that people must take a position relative to specific claims made in the spirit of communication and understanding, there are myriad ways in which communication breaks down. As Ross and Stillinger (1991) have observed, there are both strategic and psychological barriers to dispute resolution. In many instances, the speakers' are unwilling or unable to accept terms that might lead to agreement. Such limitations may be beyond the participants' conscious awareness-revealing ideological obstacles to communicative understanding (Bahktin, 1986). This is true, even in the evaluation of ostensibly objective scientific data such as remote staring. This is ironic given that a deeper reading of the discourse finds common forms and rhetorical styles that reveal a shared speech community that could lead to shared meaning and interpretation.

As I offer a critique of the psi research discourse, I include my own view as both a participant and an observer. Over the past 25 years, I have been an active researcher in the field, collecting data on remote staring and other psi related phenomena. I know most of the principal actors within the debate and have been actively involved as an advocate for research in this area. This position provides a vantage point from which to view the style and content of the controversy, as well as some of the personal tensions and frustrations that I have experienced. In this process I am engaged in a form of what Stewart (1991) referred to as 'contaminated critique' — exposing the limitations of dichotomies between subjective and objective ways of knowing — as well as the arbitrary nature of categories such as 'sceptic' and 'proponent'.

In my own research on remote staring, I have been engaged directly in the debate over valid knowledge and valid ways of knowing. In two formal experiments, I found statistically significant evidence for a remote staring effect using close circuit television, objective measures of autonomic nervous system activity, and the use of a randomized, double blind protocol (Schlitz and Laberge, 1994). My colleague, Richard Wiseman (a card carrying member of the sceptical community) conducted similar experiments and found chance results in his laboratory (Wiseman and Smith, 1994; Wiseman et al., 1995). Based on these differences under similar experimental protocols, we decided to conduct a joint study. We carried out two identical experiments making use of the same equipment, same radomization, same subject population. The only difference was that Wiseman or I did the staring. In these experiments, we each replicated our initial findings (Wiseman and Schlitz, 1997). The unusual effect was further replicated in a second collaborative study, in which we again replicated our original findings (Wiseman and Schlitz, 1998). A third collaboration, which pushed both investigators far beyond our boredom threshold, found no overall significance to support the remote staring hypothesis (Schlitz et al., 2005). How do we walk away from these confusing results? Can we reach a firm conclusion from our studies about the existence of remote staring or the nature of the experimenter effect which seems to stand in the face of objective truth claims made within the paradigm of randomized, double blind conditions? Certainty is obscured by the equivocal results. And yet, both Wiseman and I have confirmation for our original positions — I found significance in 4 out of 5 studies, while he found it in none. Despite this, our collaboration speaks to the value of cooperation between alternative positions and between holders of different truth claims. Our collaboration speaks to a playing field in which open discourse is possible, even in the face of competing data. Good will, mutual respect, and an open minded search for truth can be addressed when we move beyond rhetorical posturing that polarizes more than it informs.

By positing an ideal speech situation, we increase our awareness of the specific factors that constitute direct and indirect manipulations of consciousness (White, 1988). This vantage point links structural constraints within the scientific establishment with everyday dialogues between scientists of differing orientations. I believe we really have more in common than we might think. More opportunities to find a middle ground may reveal important insights into the epistemological and ontological implications of psi phenomena for understanding the nature of truth in western culture.

References

Alcock, J.A., Burns, J.E. & Freeman, A. (ed. 2002), *Psi Wars: Getting to Grips with the Paranormal* (Exeter: Imprint Academic; Special Issue of *Journal of Consciousness Studies* on Parapsychology).

Bakhtin, M.M. (1986), *Speech Genres and Other Late Essays,* translated by Vem McGee and edited by Caryl Emerson and Michael Holquist (Austin, TX: University of Texas).

Gieryn, Thomas (1983), 'Boundary-work and the demarcation of science from non-science: strains and interests in professional ideologies of scientists', *American Sociological Review,* **48**, pp. 781–95.

Habermas, Jurgen (1970), 'Toward a theory of communicative competence', in *Patterns of Communicative Behavior,* ed. H. Dreitzel (New York: Macmillan).

Habermas, Jurgen (1971), *Knowledge and Human Interests,* translated by J. Shapiro (Boston, MA: Beacon Press).

Habermas, Jurgen (1979), *Communication and the Evolution of Society,* translated by T. McCarthy (Boston, MA: Beacon Press).

Habermas, Jurgen (1981), *The Theory of Communicative Action, vol.1, Reason and Rationalization of Society,* translated by T. McCarthy (Boston, MA: Beacon Press).

Hess, David (1993), *Science in the NewAge: The Paranormal, Its Defenders and Debunkers, and American Culture* (Madison, WI: University of Wisconsin).

Jastrow, Joseph (1900), *Fact and Fable in Psychology* (Boston, MA: Houghton, Mifflin, and Co.).

Mauskopf, Seymour and McVaugh, Michael (1980), *The Elusive Science. Origins of Experimental Psychical Research* (Baltimore, MD: Johns Hopkins University).

McClenon, James (1984), *Deviant Science: The Case of Parapsychology* (Philadelphia, PA: University of Pennslvania Press).

Ross, Lee and Stillinger, Constance (1991), 'Barriers to conflict resolution', *Negotiation Journal*, **8**, pp. 389–403.

Schiffrin, Deborah (1987), *Discourse Markers* (Cambridge: Cambridge University Press).

Schlitz, M. and Laberge, S. (1994), 'Autonomic detection of remote observation: Two conceptual replications', in *Proceedings of Presented Papers 37th Annual Parapsychological Association Convention*, ed. D.J. Bierman (Fairhaven, MA: Parapsychological Association).

Schlitz, M., Wiseman, R., Radin, D. and Watts, C. (2005), 'Of two minds: Skeptic–proponent collaboration in parapsychology', *Proceedings of the Parapsychological Association Convention* (in press).

Snow, C.P. (1959), *Two Cultures and the Scientific Revolution* (New York: Cambridge University Press).

Wiseman, R. and Schlitz, M. (1997), 'Experimenter effects and the remote detection of staring', *Journal of Parapsychology*, **61**, pp. 197–207.

Wiseman, R. and Schlitz, M. (1998), 'Further studies of experimenter effects and the remote detection of staring', *Proceedings of the Parapsychological Association*.

Wiseman, R. and Smith, M. (1994), 'A further look at the detection of unseen gaze', *Proceedings of the Parapsychological Association*, pp. 465–78.

Wiseman, R., Smith, M., Freedman, D., Wasserman, T. and Hurst, C. (1995), 'Examining the remote staring effect. Two further experiments', *Proceedings of the Presented papers, Parapsychological Association, 38th Annual Convention*, pp. 480–90.

White, Stephen K. (1988), *The Recent Work of Jurgen Habermas: Reason, Justice, and Modernity* (Cambridge: Cambridge University Press).

STEFAN SCHMIDT

Comments on Sheldrake's 'The Sense of Being Stared At'

In the first part of his contribution Rupert Sheldrake gives an overview on the empirical situation regarding 'the sense of being stared at' that results in an optimistic and positive statement about the phenomenon under consideration. Although I am open-minded (but not convinced) regarding the phenomenon, I shall set out to demonstrate that a lot of the empirical material brought forward by Sheldrake is not that conclusive. I will do so with the intention of eliciting more conclusive research in order to better understand this fascinating phenomenon. But before I do so I will make a few comments on the context in which Sheldrake's activities are taking place.

Rupert Sheldrake has his own style of research which differs from how scientific investigations are usually run. One of the main differences is that its science mostly addresses rather the lay public than other scientists. He has written many popular books about unsolved problems in science, he often gives talks to the interested lay public and he is presenting a lot of his research in the media. But it is not only about presenting; Sheldrake also collects his data in a more public way than it is custom for normal science. His experiments often take place in schools, in a TV setting, or he suggests conducting experiments within science museums. In his books and on his website he encourages people to conduct their own experiments. Sheldrake provides them with the adequate material, randomization lists, online experiments, instructions, data sheet and the like. He suggested recently (Sheldrake, 2004) distributing one per cent of the money spent in science according to the (democratic) wishes of the general public.

Sheldrake continually tries to bridge the large gap between what is taking place in the laboratories and its public perception. His intentions are not only to explain the complicated to the lay people but also to bring the interests of the public back to science. Sheldrake is advocating research into unexplained phenomena that are widely neglected within mainstream science. His democratic approach targets the problem that scientists usually research what normal people do not understand or are not interested in, but avoid investigating those phenomena which puzzle people in their daily lives. The 'sense of being stared at' is only one example, and it could equally well have been precognitive dreaming, telepathic experiences or synchronistic events. By inviting lay people to perform the experiments which professionals refuse to conduct, he briliantly exposes a wide spread dogma within science. This dogma defines which topics are rightly viewed as belonging to science and which ones are to be regarded as superstitious beliefs and thus are not worth considering. The important point to be made here is that this dogma is itself an unproven belief. Science is defined not by its topic but by its methodological (i.e. scientific) approach. This is a fact which many scientists still refuse to acknowledge.

So is the solution to the widespread neglect of investigations into the paranormal that these are researched by school children? The answer is yes and no! Yes, because this public pressure does not leave science unimpressed. It advocates a change which is needed urgently. No, because most of the data conducted within these public experiments cannot replace good controlled research in the laboratory. If the aim is to nail down 'the sense of being stared at' as a fact then these data will never be sufficient. Such field studies and public experiments are just one part of several approaches that will be needed. Only a multiplicity of approaches all targeting the same phenomenon will succeed in the long run. Sheldrake constantly errs when he argues that his own material is a conclusive proof for the existence of 'the sense of being stared at'. Of course, as an advocate of a neglected public opinion he has to do so. But this is more a political statement than one based on evidence. In my view Sheldrake no longer has any choice but to discuss the data from a more or less neutral point of view. Therefore he is missing parts of the story.

Experiments taking place on a large scale in public, like the staring experiments published by Sheldrake, lack the important controls which allow the conclusion that any effect found in the data is due to the variable under consideration and is not an artifact of any other influences or circumstances. Most of these problems are already mentioned in his paper: sensory cueing, scoring errors, cheating and the like. I would agree with Sheldrake that none of these artifacts are solely responsible for his average hit rate of 54.7% (Mean chance expectation 50%). But can't it result from a mixture of them? Some kids are cheating because they want to present positive results to the investigator, others get confused with the notation (if you don't stare and the other person says 'not stared' you have to denote a hit), and others again are helped by some subtle cues nobody (including themselves) is aware of. All these things happen every now and then and everybody who has ever conducted such experiments will be aware of the fact that these easy set-ups can get very tricky after a thorough look at all possibilities for artifacts. The introduction of precautions such as blindfold, earplugs and the elimination of direct feedback (in combination with sensory cues a possibility for learning effects) has reduced the effect from 56.8% and 54.9% to 53% in the following study. So parts of the effect might have been due to these artifacts. However, in direct comparisons in a later study (Sheldrake, 2001) no direct differences could be found for trials with and without blindfolds and with and without feedback. But to complete the picture studies with still tighter controls in a laboratory have to be performed. Public studies have the advantage of a high ecological validity; laboratory studies have the advantage of high controls (internal validity). Both approaches will contrast and complement each other in order to give a complete picture. In a laboratory sensory shielding can be handled in a far better way than in class rooms. Videotaping of the experiments allow for scoring by independent (maybe even blinded) raters to avoid cheating and scoring errors. So why not invite schoolgirls and boys to the laboratory? I even suggest inviting only those kids who had positive scores in order to find out whether they can repeat their success.

At this point, where Sheldrake can already report more than 30,000 trials conducted in the field, we need more input at the better controlled end of the scale, i.e. rigorously conducted high quality laboratory studies.

But unfortunately Sheldrake is following the opposite direction. He promotes a completely uncontrolled online test where everybody who is looking for fun can enter via the internet some invented data without even performing the experiment. I gave this test a try with a colleague in my office. Twice I got confused with the 'correct', 'not correct', 'stare' and 'do not stare' commands and I entered a false positive result. The software (which does not run with every browser) allowed me to go back and to enter a second result for the trials. After twenty trials I had twenty-two results! Then after pressing the send data button I could see that only my wrong results where transmitted. Thus the data reported in this journal already contain my erroneous (and thus positive!) data although I did not set out with the intention to cheat. Such an online test has no scientific value at all! The opposite is true: everybody who has seen this low quality test will take a more sceptical view of other data produced by the author. There is definitely no need for more uncontrolled data but for more controlled trials! Only these are able to rule out the artifact hypotheses.

Finally I would like to comment on the research patterns in these staring trials. Sheldrake often presents his results separated for looking trials and non looking trials. In most of the cases hit rates in the looking trials are higher than in non-looking trials. At several places (e.g. Sheldrake, 1999; 2003) he concludes from this pattern that staring is better detected than non-staring and that this might be due to an evolutionary reason which in turn is a proof of the effect. But this cannot be concluded from this data as splitting the data between looking and non-looking trials without taking the response pattern of the participants into account leads to wrong conclusions. There are many simple statistical ways to take this response pattern into account (see e.g. Burdick & Kelly, 1977; Radin, 2004). Figures like nos 1–4 in Sheldrake's paper give the impression that people perform differently in looking and not looking trials. But probably they don't. Such figures should always be contrasted with figures where the hit rates for the two possible answers 'Yes, I was stared at' and 'No, I was not stared at' are presented. Only this additional pattern will complete the picture.

In all of these experiments people report more often that they were stared at than that they were not stared at. This might be due to some internal bias which has nothing to do with a staring experience. Maybe people just tend to say 'yes' rather than 'no'. This response bias would then distribute evenly on the stare and non-stare trials. But it might also be that people report more positive answer because they sense the gaze from behind. It is not true that these two hypotheses cannot be differentiated statistically (as claimed in Sheldrake's paper). The relevant test is fairly easy. If the participants really sense the gaze better than the non-gazing then they should get a higher hit rate for the trials where they report 'Yes I was stared at' vs. trials where they report 'not stared at'. If the response bias is evenly distributed the two hit rates should be the same. Table 5 in Sheldrake (1999) gives a grand total of 13,903 trials and allows for such a calculation. If people report 'stared at' they are right in 55.1% of the cases, if they report 'not stared at' this is correct in 54.8 % of the trials. These data favour the hypotheses that the response bias is not related to the any staring experience. Radin (2004) found the same result with a different method, and Sheldrake has long been aware of this fact, but he does not report this important additional information. I would like to suggest a a simple empirical test that could resolve this matter. Usually participants complete twenty trials in a row with a more or less even number of stare or non-stare trials. If the participants don't get feedback another two sets of twenty trials each can be performed where the distribution of looking and non-looking trials is highly skewed. E.g. 18 looking trials out of twenty in the next session and then only 2 in the third one. The sequence of these three sessions has to be random with different participants. If the response pattern (number of yes/no answers) is dependent on the distant gaze then it should shift according to the frequency of the gazes. But if the bias is not related to distant staring it will be same in all three sessions.

References

Burdick, D.S. & Kelly, E.F. (1977), 'Statistical methods in parapsychological research', in *Handbook of Parapsychology*, ed. B.B. Wolman (New York: Van Nostrand Reinhold).

Radin, D.I. (2004), 'The feeling of being stared at: An analysis and replication', *Journal of the Society for Psychical Research*, **68**, pp. 246–53.

Sheldrake, R. (1999), 'The "sense of being stared at" confirmed by simple experiments', *Rivista di Biologia / Biology Forum*, **92**, pp. 53–76.

Sheldrake, R. (2001), 'Experiments on the sense of being stared at: the elimination of possible artifacts', *Journal of the Society for Psychical Research*, **65**, pp. 122–37.

Sheldrake, R. (2003), *The Sense of Being Stared At* (London: Hutchinson).

Sheldrake, R. (2004), 'Public participation: Let the people pick projects', *Nature*, **432**, p. 271.

MAX VELMANS

Are We Out of Our Minds?

We experience physical objects as being out in the world, not in our heads or brains. Although we might accept that there are neural causes, neural correlates and neural representations of those perceived objects in our brains, we do not *experience* them as being in our brains. This is deeply puzzling, and has been a source of debate for philosophers and scientists for around 2,500 years. As William James (1904) put it '... the whole philosophy of perception from Democritus's time downwards has been just one long wrangle over the paradox that what is evidently one reality should be in two places at once, both in outer space and in a person's mind'.

At first glance, one might not notice what the fuss is about, given that a common, naïve realist way of dealing with this paradox is to assume that what we see out in space is the *object itself* and that we have an additional, veridical experience *of* that object in our brains. Why is this form of realism naïve?

Firstly, because science tells us that the perceived colour, shape, location in phenomenal space and other visual features of an object are just surface *representations* of what the object is like, constructed by our visual systems. A microscope is all that is needed to convince one that these surface appearances are not all there is to an object. These surface appearances are also very different to the descriptions of the deeper structure of those objects and the space in which they are embedded given by physics, for example by relativity theory and quantum mechanics. So, although we normally think of the *perceived object* as the 'physical object' it is nevertheless how that object *looks to us*, and not how it is *in itself.*[10] Similarly, although we normally think of the 3D phenomenal space in which the perceived object is embedded as 'physical space', it too is how space looks to us rather than space itself. Note that it follows from this that while perceived objects are in one sense 'physical' they are in another sense 'psychological' (they are appearances constructed by our visual systems).

Secondly, we *don't* have any experience of the object in our brains *in addition* to the object as perceived out in the world. The perceived objects *are* what we experience — and in terms of their *phenomenology*, an object as perceived and our experience *of* the object are one and the same. When looking at this print, for example, the print that one sees out here on the page is the only 'print experience' that one has. So naïve realism is wrong in two ways — it is neither consistent with third-person science, nor first-person experience.

How then are we to make sense of the fact that objects seem to be 'out there' while our brains and what they contain are, so to speak, 'over here'? As Sheldrake (Part 2) points out in his fascinating review of ancient and modern thinking on this subject, theories of vision have ranged from 'extramissive' theories that posit some active influence emanating from the eyes that both illuminates and influences the external world, 'intramissive' theories that stress the

---

[10] I give a full analysis of how phenomenal features and theory-driven physical descriptions relate to each other and to the thing itself in Velmans (2000) ch7.

influence of the external world on the (passive) brain, and theories in which intramissive and extramissive influences combine. As Sheldrake notes, up to the twelfth century, extramissive theories were dominant, but with an increasing understanding of the way light reflected from an object is focused on the retina by the lens of the eye, intramissive theories have become dominant. While Kepler's theory of vision stopped at the retina, modern investigations of vision have extended this understanding considerably into what is going on in the depths of the brain, in terms of visual feature analysis, the way different regions of the brain combine together to form representations of the object, the areas of the brain involved and so on. This ongoing research programme is highly productive and we have good reasons to hope that, in time, it will yield a good understanding of what it investigates: the neural causal antecedents of visual experiences (the necessary and sufficient preceding neural conditions) and the NCC — the neural correlates of given conscious experiences.

But that isn't the full story of perception. What about the experiences themselves? It is well accepted that one cannot directly observe another's first-person experience by a third-person investigation of their brain, and it goes without saying that the antecedent causes of experiences are not the experiences themselves (causes should not be confused with their *effects*). Nor should we confuse experiences with their neural correlates. Even if we found that each unique experience is accompanied in 1:1 fashion by a unique set of neural correlates, we could not conclude that those first person experiences were nothing more than those correlates. The relationship would of course be intimate, but the apparent differences in third-person *neural* features and first-person *phenomenal* features would remain. One might for example know all there was to know (from a third-person perspective) about the neural features without knowing anything about the accompanying phenomenal features, unless one had already established this neural/phenomenal correspondence by combining neural investigations with first person phenomenological reports. If so, an exclusively third-person account of perception cannot be complete.[11] For completeness, one has to add a veridical description of first-person perceptual *effects*.

This was the motivation for the reflexive model of perception that I introduced in Velmans (1990) and developed into a more general Reflexive Monist account of how consciousness relates to the brain and the physical world in Velmans (2000) — see Figure 1 below.

This (highly schematised) model starts in the conventional way with a third-person account of the stimulus, in this case, a cat as perceived by an external observer. Light rays reflected from the cat's surface activate the subject's visual

---

[11] To get over this problem, physicalist and functionalist theories of consciousness have tried to argue that, in spite of their apparent differences, experiences are nothing more than (are ontologically identical to) their neural causes and/or physical or functional correlates. However, the formal differences between causation, correlation, and ontological identity in terms of symmetry and Leibniz's law blocks this reduction. Given that third person science is *restricted* to the discovery of neural causes and correlates, this block cannot be removed by any conceivable third-person investigation of the brain, forming a major stumbling block for third-person reductionism that is seldom addressed, and, to my knowledge, has never been overcome (see full discussion in Velmans, 1998a, 2000 ch3).

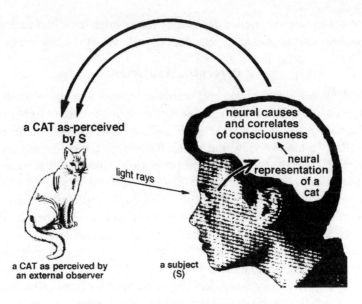

Figure 1. A reflexive model of perception

system, producing neural representations in the occipital and associated regions of her brain. If the subject experiences the cat, the neural causes and correlates of that experience also form in her brain. That is where the (intromissive) third-person story ends. The reflexive model then adds what the subject actually experiences to the model, namely a phenomenal cat out in the world. Central to the model is the recognition that an entity in the external world is (reflexively) experienced by the subject to be a phenomenal object in the external world — not in the brain, as reductionism would have it, and not 'in the soul' as the ancients supposed — in the same way that this print is seen to be out here on this page. In short, when attending to the cat, the subject experiences more or less what the external observer experiences when he looks at the cat. The subject just sees it from a different angle.

The same of course applies to other phenomenal objects and events that, together with the perceived space in which they are embedded, make up the external phenomenal world. Where are these phenomenal objects and events? Out in the phenomenal world. The phenomenal cat in Figure 1 is out in the phenomenal world, a pain in the foot is in the experienced foot, and this perceived print on this visible page really is out here on this page. Technically, this is a form of *phenomenological externalism*,[12] which immediately presents us with the problem of *perceptual projection*: given that the proximal neural causes and

---

[12] To relate the reflexive model to Sheldrake's analysis, I will focus on phenomena that have such apparent external location and extension, but the reflexive model is not externalist (for any doctrinal reason) about all experiences. Whether an experience is located in external phenomenal space, on the body surface, inside the head, or nowhere, is an empirical matter that is entirely dependent on its phenomenology. For example, the phonemic imagery that accompanies the thought that 2+2=4 does not have a clear location, or might seem, at best, to be roughly located inside the head (see Velmans, 2000, ch. 6).

correlates of what we experience *are* in the head or brain, how can we explain the fact that various sensations and experienced objects seem to be beyond the brain?

I: Perceptual Projection

As Sheldrake notes, this is an ancient problem, and one ancient solution was that some extromissive physical influence emanates from the eyes to light up or other wise influence the world. Given the evidence from staring experiments in his target paper (Part 1), this is a view that Sheldrake himself adopts in his Part 2. In the reflexive model, however, 'perceptual projection' simply refers to an *empirically observable effect*, for example, to the fact that this print seems to be out here on this page and not in your brain. In short, perceptual projection is an effect that requires explanation; perceptual projection is not itself an explanation. We know that preconscious processes within the brain produce consciously experienced events that may be subjectively located and extended in the phenomenal space beyond the brain, but we don't really know how this is done. We also know that this effect is subjective, psychological and viewable only from a first-person perspective. In the reflexive model, nothing *physical* is assumed to project from the brain.[13] This raises a vexing question: some experiences might *seem* to be beyond the brain, but if they are not physically 'projected', are such experiences really where they seem?

II: How Phenomenal Space Relates to Real Space

No one doubts that physical bodies can have real extension and location in space. Dualists and reductionists nevertheless find it hard to accept that experiences can have a real, as opposed to a 'seeming' location and extension. They do not doubt, for example, that a physical foot has a real location and extension in space, but, for them, a pain in the foot can't really be in the foot, as they are committed to the view that it is either nowhere or in the brain. For them, location in phenomenal space is not location in real space. According to the reflexive model however, this ignores the fact that, in everyday life, we take the phenomenal world to *be* the physical world. It also ignores the pivotal role of phenomenal space in forming our very understanding of space, and with it, our understanding of location and extension in measured or 'real' space.

What we normally think of as the 'physical foot' for example is actually the *phenomenal foot* (the foot as seen, felt and so on). That does not stop us from pointing to it, measuring its location and extension and so on. If so, at least some phenomenal objects can be measured. While a pain in the foot might not be measurable with the same precision, few would doubt that we could specify its rough location and extension (and differentiate it for example from a pain in the back).

---

[13] Although we don't have a full understanding of how perceptual projection works, there is a large experimental literature about the information that is used by the brain to model distance and location. There are also many ways to demonstrate perceptual projection in action, for example in hallucinations, phantom limbs, stereoscopic pictures, holograms, and virtual realities. I have discussed this literature elsewhere, along with some potentially useful models to explain it (holography and virtual reality) in Velmans (1990; 1993; 1998b; 2000).

What we normally think of as 'space' also refers, at least in the initial instance, to the phenomenal space that we experience through which we appear to move. Our intuitive understanding of spatial location and extension, for example, derives in the first instance from the way objects and events appear to be arranged relative to each other in phenomenal space (closer, further, behind, in front, left, right, bigger, smaller and so on). We are also accustomed to making size and distance estimates based on such appearances. This print for example appears to be out here in front of my face, and THIS PRINT appears to be bigger than this print. However, we recognise that these ordinal judgments are only rough and ready ones, so when we wish to establish 'real' location, distance, size or some other spatial attribute, we usually resort to some form of *measurement* that quantifies the dimensions of interest using an arbitrary but agreed metric (feet, metres etc.), relative to some agreed frame of reference (for example a Cartesian frame of reference with an agreed zero point from which measurement begins). The correspondence, or lack of correspondence, between phenomenal space and measured space is assessed in the same way, by comparing distance judgments with distance measurements in psychology experiments. For example, I can estimate the distance of this phenomenal print from my nose, but I can also place one end of a measuring tape on the tip of my nose (point zero) and the other end on this print to determine its real distance.

Such comparisons allow one to give a broad specification of how well phenomenal space corresponds to or maps onto measured space. There are of course alternative representations of space suggested by physics (four-dimensional space–time, the 11 dimensional space of string theory, etc.) and non-Cartesian geometries (e.g. Riemann geometry). However, a comparison of phenomenal to measured (Cartesian) space is all that we need to decide whether a pain in my foot or this perceived print on this page is, or is not, really in my brain. According to the reflexive model, phenomenal space provides a natural representation, shaped by evolution, of the distance and location of objects viewed from the perspective of the embodied observer, which models real distance and location quite well at close distances, where accuracy is important for effective interaction with the world. My estimate that this page is about 0.5 metres from my nose, for example, is not far off. However, phenomenal appearances and our consequent distance judgments quickly lose accuracy as distances increase. For example, the dome of the night sky provides the outer boundary of the phenomenal world, but gives a completely misleading representation of distances in stellar space.

Note that, although we can use measuring instruments to correct unaided judgments of apparent distance, size and so on, measuring tapes and related instruments themselves appear to us as phenomenal objects, and *measurement operations appear to us as operations that we are carrying out on phenomenal objects in phenomenal space*. In short, even our understanding of 'real' or measured location is underpinned by our experience of phenomenal location. And crucially, whether I make distance judgments about this perceived print and judge it to be around 0.5 metres in front of my face, or measure it to find that it is only 0.42 metres, *does not alter the phenomenon that I am judging or measuring*.

The distance of the print that I am judging or measuring is the distance of this perceived print out here on this visible page, not some *other* 'physical print' in some *other* 'physical space', and not some other 'experience of print' in my brain.

III: Paradigm Clash

In recent years the spatially extended nature of much of conscious experience (in the form of an experienced phenomenal world) has been increasingly accepted in the psychological and brain sciences, and its implications for an understanding of consciousness has once more become a topical issue. For example, Karl Pribram (1971; 2004), one of the first scientists to address this problem, has continued to develop his earlier theories of holographic representation as an explanatory model of how consciousness relates to brain; Antti Revonsuo (1995) developed the suggestion that the phenomenal world is a form of virtual reality (see also Velmans, 1990; 1993; 1998b); and Steven Lehar (2003) has attempted to develop a mathematical model of how objects *appear* as they move in phenomenal space (as opposed to how they really *are* as they move in phenomenal space). As these, and other scientists (such as Jeffrey Gray, 2004) have pointed out, the 3D nature of the phenomenal world is likely to have important consequences for neuroscience, for the obvious reason that the brain has to be organised in a way that supports such spatially extended experiences.

These theorists nevertheless remain divided on the issue of whether some of these experiences are outside the brain. Pribram (2004) takes the view that they are, and develops a broad theory of perception that he explicitly links to the reflexive monism developed in Velmans (2000). By contrast, Revonsuo, Lehar and Gray adopt an intromissive form of biological naturalism, arguing that the entire 3D phenomenal world, stretching to the horizon and the dome of the sky, is a form of virtual reality that is literally located inside the brain. For them, this ultimately reduces the problems of consciousness to problems of neurophysiology — a reduction that Lehar claims to be more 'scientific' than the notion of perceptual projection. However, Lehar (2003) also points out that biological naturalism forces one into a surprising conclusion: if the phenomenal world is inside the brain, the real skull must be outside the phenomenal world (the former and the latter are logically equivalent).

Let me be clear: if one accepts that

(a) The phenomenal world appears to have spatial extension to the perceived horizon and dome of the sky.
(b) The phenomenal world is literally inside the brain.

It follows that

(c) The real skull (as opposed to the phenomenal skull) is beyond the perceived horizon and dome of the sky.

Although Lehar accepts this conclusion, he admits that this consequence of biological naturalism is 'incredible'. I agree, and, in my view, this casts an entirely different light on the so-called 'scientific' status of biological naturalism and the so-called 'unscientific' status of perceptual projection (in the reflexive model). Decide for yourself. Put your hands on your head. Is that the real skull that you feel, located more or less where it seems to be? If that makes sense, the reflexive model makes sense. Or is that just a phenomenal skull inside your brain, with your real skull beyond the dome of the sky? If the latter seems absurd, biological naturalism is absurd.

Note that the differences between reflexive monism (RM) and biological naturalism (BN) largely hinge on how they conceive the nature of the 'brain'. RM adopts critical realism — the conventional view that, although our experiences do not give us a full representation of how things really are, they normally provide useful approximations. As a first approximation, 'brains' are what one finds inside the skulls that we feel sitting on the top of our necks, that one can find pictures of in neurophysiological textbooks, and that are occasionally to be seen pickled in jars. Although I accept that these 'brains' are really phenomenal brains, these mental models are roughly accurate. Consequently, the location and extension of the phenomenal and real brain closely correspond.

Lehar also accepts that phenomenal brains are mental models of real ones, but BN forces him to claim that the real skull is beyond the perceived dome of the sky. If so, our assumption that the real brain is more or less where it seems to be (inside the perceived skull) must be a delusion. The alternative is that biological naturalism is wrong. Not only is the notion of a skull beyond the perceived universe unfalsifiable (it would always be beyond any phenomena that one could actually perceive), but it is also hard to know in what sense something that *surrounds* the perceived universe could be a 'skull' (it certainly isn't the skull that we can feel on top of our necks). Nor is it easy to grasp in what sense something that *contains* the perceived universe is a 'brain' (it certainly isn't the brain that one can perceive inside the skulls on top of our necks).

IV: Paradigm Convergence: Are We Out of Our Minds?

There may however be a different way of understanding some of the implications of BN and RM that allows for a measure of convergence — with some interesting links to Sheldrake's theories. BN and RM agree for example that the entire phenomenal world is part of conscious experience, and that it makes sense to suggest that there is a 'vehicle' or 'ground' of some kind that carries or contains it. As Sheldrake notes in his second paper, projective theories accept that experienced objects are in the mind, although not inside the brain. But what kind of 'mind' could contain a 3D phenomenal world? While RM adopts the conventional view that the immediate carriers of conscious experience are unconscious and preconscious mental processes within the human brain, it also accepts that the brain does not operate in isolation. Rather,

> human consciousness is embedded in and supported by the greater universe (just as the tip of the iceberg is supported by the base and the surrounding sea). The contents of human consciousness are also a natural *expression* or *manifestation* of the embedding universe. In humans, the *proximal* causes of consciousness are to be found in the human brain, but it is a mistake to think of the brain as an isolated

system. Its existence as a material system depends totally on its supporting surround, and the contents of consciousness that it, in turn, supports arise from a reflexive interaction of perceptual processing with entities, events and processes in the surrounding world, body and the mind/brain itself (Velmans, 2000, p. 229).

In a broader sense, then, the universe itself *both* contains the objects and events within it *and* our conscious experiences of those objects and events — and in this special sense the universe itself might be thought of as the supporting vehicle, ground, or 'mind'.

How does this relate to findings from staring experiments? RM provides a way to unify a range of phenomena (the 3D phenomenal world, hallucinations, virtual realities, etc.), and their consequences for understanding consciousness, but Sheldrake is right to note that it makes no predictions about the extromissive influences that staring experiments suggest. However, if these influences do exist, RM does indicate where one might look for them. Conscious experiences arise from unconscious and preconscious processes in the mind/brain interacting with the surrounding world. So if there are connections between human individuals of the kind suggested by staring experiments, it is in the unconscious processes that support conscious experience rather than in the phenomenology of experience itself that one should look. If bi-directional information flows operate unconsciously, that would explain the finding that skin resistance measures indicate stare detection more sensitively than subjects' verbal reports — and it would also make sense of the fact that one might 'feel' another's focused attention without having any knowledge of how that feeling comes about. Bi-directional information flows of this kind could then be thought of as properties of an extended, unconscious mind.

Time will tell. But let us suppose that such unconscious connections between individuals are found to exist. Would that mean we are out of our minds? Not really. If such interconnections were found, we would be *in* our minds — but partly out of our brains.

References

Gray, J. (2004), *Consciousness: Creeping Up On The Hard Problem* (Oxford: OUP).

Lehar, S. (2003), 'Gestalt isomorphism and the primacy of subjective conscious experience: A gestalt bubble model', *Behavioral & Brain Sciences*, **26** (4), pp. 375–444.

Pribram, K.H. (1971), *Languages of the Brain: Experimental Paradoxes and Principles in Neuropsychology* (New York: Brandon House).

Pribram, K. (2004), 'Consciousness reassessed', *Mind and Matter*, **2** (1), 7–35.

Revonsuo, A. (1995), 'Consciousness, dreams, and virtual realities', *Philosophical Psychology*, **8** (1), pp. 35–58.

Velmans, M. (1990), 'Consciousness, brain, and the physical world', *Philosophical Psychology*, **3**, pp. 77–99.

Velmans, M.(1993), 'A reflexive science of consciousness', in *Experimental and Theoretical Studies of Consciousness. CIBA Foundation Symposium 174* (Chichester: Wiley).

Velmans, M. (1998a), 'Goodbye to reductionism', in *Towards a Science of Consciousness II: The Second Tucson Discussions and Debates*, ed. S.Hameroff, A.Kaszniak & A.Scott (Cambridge, MA: MIT Press).

Velmans, M. (1998b), 'Physical, psychological and virtual realities', in *The Virtual Embodied*, ed. J. Wood (London: Routledge).

Velmans, M. (2000), *Understanding Consciousness* (London: Routledge/Psychology Press).

Rupert Sheldrake

The Non-Visual Detection of Staring

Response to Commentators

I am grateful to all who have commented on my papers in this issue of *JCS*. This discussion has helped clarify terminology; it has pointed towards improved experimental methods and statistics; it has illuminated the nature of 'normal' theories of vision and the alternatives; and it has suggested directions for further research.

I: Terminology

Several people found the 'sense of being stared at' too vague. Susan Blackmore pointed out that it could include the uncontroversial ability of animals to see when others' gazes are directed towards them. As other respondents realized, the 'sense of being stared at' was intended to mean an ability to detect looks from behind, outside the range of vision. But Blackmore is right to insist that this distinction is made explicit. A phrase such as 'non-visual' should be added to the 'sense of being stared at'.

William Braud questioned whether the word 'sense' is appropriate. In many cases, he pointed out, the detection of staring may indeed be accompanied by a feeling, and also by physiological changes, justifying the term 'sense'; but in other cases it may involve behavioural reactions, such as turning around, without any conscious awareness of being stared at. Also, he suggested, there might be a form of 'direct knowing' rather than sensing. He argued that 'staring detection' is a more accurate term. I agree.

Anthony Atkinson also questioned the use of the term 'sense' on the grounds that such a sense would be very primitive if it conveyed only one message, namely 'someone is staring at me'. But although most tests carried out so far have concentrated on yes/no responses, there may well be more to this ability. People often claim to detect the direction from which a stare is coming; some people seem able to detect which part of their body is being stared at; and different emotions or intentions associated with a stare may have different effects, according to people's reports of their experiences (Sheldrake, 2003). I discuss in

Journal of Consciousness Studies, **12**, No. 6, 2005, pp. 117–26

Section V experiments to test people's ability to discriminate between stares directed at different parts of the body.

Ian Baker favoured the term 'remote staring detection', but while this is appropriate for CCTV tests, it does not apply to the detection of staring at fairly close range, as in direct looking tests.

'Non-visual staring detection' seems the most neutral and inclusive phrase, although it is rather clumsy. A new scientific term is needed, and Roger Carpenter's proposal of *scopaesthesia* (in American spelling, scopesthesia) seems the best candidate. Scopaesthesia's roots are the Greek verb *skopein*, to look at, as in microscope and telescope, and *aesthesis*, sensation, as in anaesthesia (no sensation) and kinaesthesia (sensation of movement). The pronunciation of 'scop' should be with a short o, as in 'shop'.

If scopaesthesia only implied feeling or sensation, it might run foul of Braud's objection to the term 'sense', but in scientific terminology aesthesia implies both sensation and detection. For example, in the *Penguin Dictionary of Biology*, 'kinaesthetic' is defined as 'detecting movement'. I will henceforth use the word scopaesthesia to mean non-visual staring detection.

II: Data and Statistics

The meta-analysis by Dean Radin revealed more clearly and more quantitatively than my own review of the data that the direct staring experiments show a highly significant effect, unlikely to be explicable in terms of subliminal cues. Some respondents suggested that the effects could be due to the selective reporting of positive outcomes, but Radin quantified this possible file-drawer effect and showed that to negate the overall positive results, there would have to be 1,417 to 7,729 missing studies with null or negative effects, involving 800,000 to 3,000,000 missing trials. This seems implausible.

Carpenter claimed that 'it is difficult for an unbiased enquirer not to conclude that scopaesthesia is an illusion,' but to arrive at this conclusion he made a seemingly arbitrary selection of just five publications, and then took a majority vote which came out three to two against. His five selected studies excluded my own, but included Coover's (1913) with subjects and lookers in close proximity, and with data that showed a positive effect when analysed by the sign method (my paper 1, Figure 3). He classified Coover's as a negative study, as he did the study by Colwell *et al.* (2000) in which the first experiment showed highly significant positive results (my paper 1, Figure 4).

Jean Burns adopted an attitude of extreme caution, casting doubt on the CCTV studies on the grounds that in some of them 'the methods used to measure the EDA in these experiments were not completely up to date with current psychophysiological methods'. In the direct looking trials, she drew attention to possible problems with different randomisation methods and possible 'matching biases' in the subjects' responses. She made it sound as if all possible experimental designs could be problematic: 'At present there is no agreement as to what randomisation procedures should be used.'

Atkinson questioned the very possibility of a staring signal on two grounds. One was that a staring signal cannot be measured independently of a subjective report. But this argument would surely rule out much normal research in psychology, including research on pain. His second objection was that such a signal is 'far outside the realms of current scientific knowledge'. This is a generic argument for conservatism, but has nothing to do with question of whether such a signal exists. But despite these reservations, Atkinson helpfully pointed out how the data for the staring trials could be analysed using signal detection theory, by comparing the overall hit rate and the overall false alarm rate. He showed that the discriminability index (d') observed in staring trials was small compared with some unrelated observations from research in psychology. But the observations he referred to were made with selected subjects, whereas in practically all these staring trials, unselected samples were tested. If scopaesthesia is real, d' should be higher if sensitive subjects were selected for these tests. This is testable.

Surprisingly, Atkinson then argued that the data could have arisen from a response bias if some subjects suffered from 'delusional ideation and schizotypy personality style'. But if subjects were biased in favour of saying they were being stared at, they would have scored more than 50% in looking trials and correspondingly less than 50% in not-looking trials, with an overall hit rate of 50%, in the absence of any genuine staring detection. This is not what happened.

Stefan Schmidt wrote that I claimed that my own material 'is a conclusive proof for the existence of the "sense of being stared at"'. But I never made this claim. He then set out to cast doubt on the conclusiveness of this proof. I agree with Schmidt that more evidence is needed, and I agree that the best procedure would be to identify high scoring subjects in preliminary tests and then test them under more rigorous conditions that exclude all possible sensory cues.

As I discussed in my first paper in this issue, Schmidt and I differ in our interpretation of the pattern of data in looking and not-looking trials (my paper 1, Figures 1,3 and 4). But we agree that this question could be investigated empirically, as discussed in Section V.

III: The Intromission Paradigm

The commentary of Blackmore and the remarks of Christof Koch, quoted in the Editor's introduction, claim that 'normal' or 'scientific' theories of vision must by definition be intromission theories. Carpenter refers to this approach as 'axiomatic'. The intromission theory is one of the most venerable theories in science, dating back to the early seventeenth century. Various quantum mechanical approaches at first sight seem to open up the possibility of two-way processes in vision, but Christopher Clarke argued that these are not real alternatives.

Even Max Velmans' perceptual projection theory is 'normal' or 'scientific' in the sense that he claims that perceptual projection is non-physical, and therefore does not violate the intromission theory in a literal sense, even if it violates it in spirit.

Most commentaries also made it clear that if scopaesthesia is real then it would be incompatible with these normal theories. As Carpenter put it, 'If incontrovertible evidence could be found that scopesthesia actually existed, then that would indeed rule out a number of "scientific" theories of consciousness.' Although 'right-minded scientists', to use Carpenter's phrase, might wish for convincing disproof of scopaesthesia, the CSICOP Fellows who investigated it failed to come up with such disproof. Some of the results from their laboratories were positive, like those of Blackmore's student Jonathan James, whose work Blackmore did not mention.

Some committed sceptics deny the reality of non-visual staring detection as a matter of principle, but others, including Christopher French, regard it as an open question requiring further research, as do most other commentators in this issue of *JCS*.

IV: Alternative Hypotheses

If scopaesthesia really exists, how might it be explained? Ralph Ellis suggested that it might depend on a direct body sense that is not mediated through conventional kinds of perception. As he put it, 'The body is affected by its overall interrelations with the environment; so, if we sense how our bodies have changed from one moment to the next, we may be able to guess somewhat as to what kind of environmental changes have occurred to make our bodies feel different.' Ellis did not suggest how this might work in situations where normal sensory cues were eliminated in laboratory tests, and his idea of a body sense is so general that it could include a field-mediated effect not unlike my own proposal. So it is not clear whether the body-sense hypothesis is an alternative to a field theory of scopaesthesia, or just another way of talking about it.

Braud emphasised the importance of attention and intention in staring detection, and I agree with this emphasis. He also pointed out that for the remote staring effect, a non-local effect of attention and intention appears to be involved. But he did not explain how attention and intention are capable of acting at a distance.

As Velmans pointed out, perceptual projection is an effect that requires an explanation, and projection requires some 'vehicle' or 'ground'. Steven Lehar (2003) and Jeffrey Gray (2004) proposed that the entire 3-D phenomenal world is a form of 'virtual reality' located inside the brain, but these internal virtual reality projections also require some vehicle or ground. Both Lehar and Velmans proposed a holographic-type projection process. This is in effect a field model, although neither Lehar nor Velmans regard it literally as an electromagnetic field, as in a real hologram. So the ground of the projection remains obscure. If, as Velmans maintains, the projection process is non-physical, it seems impossible to conceive how it could be related to physical processes in the brain or to the electromagnetic field of light.

Lehar thinks it is more 'scientific' to locate perceptual projection inside the brain, even though this leads to the seemingly absurd conclusion that when we look at the sky our skulls must be beyond the sky we perceive. By contrast,

Velmans locates the projection outside the head, just as it seems to be. But he is anxious not to imply that the projection occurs through the eyes, as in old-style extramission theories. In his diagram of a man looking at a cat, the phenomenal projection arises from the head (see p. 111 above, Figure 1). But surely the perceptual projection hypothesis would work best if the projection did in fact occur through the eyes. Subjectively, we experience looking at the world through our eyes rather than through the tops of our heads.

Clarke pointed out that a new way of interpreting the standard theory of vision might be unexpectedly helpful: 'On the conventional view of vision, the perceiver and object of perception are already linked together by an electromagnetic interaction (usually construed as one way), so that they are no longer self contained systems but need to be considered as a whole.' He suggested adopting a dual-aspect view of this system so that consciousness is associated with the activity of the brain and the electromagnetic field. Then part of this consciousness would be associated with the place of the object, which is of course outside the brain.

This is a striking suggestion. But a dual aspect of the electromagnetic field does not seem enough to explain the phenomena. First, in phenomena of reflection and refraction, the virtual images are not an aspect of the electromagnetic field, but split off from it into virtual space. And second, consciousness is not necessarily linked to the electromagnetic field, but selectively linked to it. Light is falling on my body from all sides, reflected from all the objects around me. I can potentially move my eyes and direct my attention towards any of these objects; only when I do so would the electromagnetic field have the dual aspect proposed by Clarke. If I turn my head and my attention sweeps through my surroundings, then this beam of attention gives a dual aspect to different parts of the electromagnetic field as my attention moves. Even without moving my eyes, attention is selective. For example, when I look at a reflection in a window, I can either concentrate on the reflection, or I can look through the window at what lies beyond. The same electromagnetic field connects my eyes to what I am seeing in both cases, but what I see depends on my attention. Perceptions are not simply an aspect of the light entering my eyes, but involve the formation of hypotheses, to use Gregory's term (1998), as illustrated by alternative interpretations of ambiguous drawings.

As everyone agrees, visual perception depends on complex patterns of activity in various regions of the brain. These enable aspects of the retinal images to be abstracted, analysed, recognised, remembered and interpreted. I propose that perceptual fields depend on this brain activity and are closely coupled to the electromagnetic field as focused on the retinas. But, as Clarke argued, to be of any explanatory value such a field would need to be more than a re-description of the phenomenon itself, a rephrasing of the laws of optics 'in reverse'. But this rephrasing not as trivial as Clarke implied.

First, visual projections take place in straight lines in three-dimensional space. Normally, this straight-line projection means that the projected image coincides with the object seen, but as a result of reflection and refraction, as Euclid showed, visual projections produce virtual images. Perceptual fields are closely coupled to the light entering the eyes and forming images on the retinas, but these fields are separable from electromagnetic fields. They are not just a way of talking about what we already know, if all we know are the electromagnetic fields of light and the activity of the brain.

The importance of virtual images is not confined to the human realm, as a result of the technology of mirrors and lenses, but inevitably goes back to the very origins of eyes. Image-forming eyes probably first appeared more than 540 million years ago, in the Cambrian, Their appearance was associated with the 'Cambrian explosion', a rapid evolution of many new forms of animal life (Parker, 2003). All these early forms of animal life were aquatic, and reflection must have been an intrinsic feature of their visual world. Any underwater animal looking obliquely upwards experiences virtual images as a result of the total internal reflection of light by the surface of the water. Virtual images must have been part of visual experience from the beginning.

Second, the laws of optics in reverse mean that just as the focussing of light on the retina involves a reduction from three dimensions to two, the projection of the perceptual field involves an expansion from two dimensions to three. This expansion into a third dimension is a necessary feature of any 'virtual reality' theory of perception. Both Lehar and Velmans use the analogy of holograms to emphasize this dimensional transition, as does Pribram (1991).

These features of perceptual fields have implications for the understanding of morphic fields in general. First, these fields can be coupled to patterns of activity in electromagnetic fields, but are also separable from them. Second, they can project virtual images in three dimensions on the basis of patterns of electromagnetic activity. Both these features help in conceiving of the way in which morphic fields interact with the patterns of electromagnetic activity not only through the eyes but elsewhere in the in the brain.

The coupling of morphic fields to patterns of electromagnetic activity and their ability to project from two dimensions to three may be important features of morphic fields in many other situations, as in the organization of cellular development by the morphic fields of morphogenesis. The virtual forms projected within and around developing cells on the basis of patterns of electromagnetic activity around membranes and inside cells may play an essential role in shaping morphogenetic processes. Even single-celled organisms, such as radiolaria and diatoms, can form complex, highly organized structures. Just switching on the right genes and making the right proteins at the right times cannot explain the complex forms of such organisms without many other influences coming into play, including the organizing activities of microtubules, which may themselves be patterned by morphogenetic fields (Sheldrake, 1988).

In his far-ranging discussion, David Fontana showed that the idea of mind fields opens up possible connections with meditational experiences and with aspects of Buddhist philosophy.

V: Further Research

The discussion in this issue has highlighted that the most important task for further research is to establish whether scopaesthesia is real or not. Probably the best approach would be to find high-scoring looker-subject pairs by testing large numbers of people, and then test these people further under suitably rigorous conditions.

Marilyn Schlitz showed how this discussion can be seen within the context of a longstanding parapsychology-sceptic debate, which she has personally engaged in with Richard Wiseman. They carried out joint experiments on staring detection that gave results that confirmed both their initial positions. Their experimental design maximized experimenter effects, and the experimenters themselves acted as starers. This approach has resulted in a stalemate.

Automated procedures, described below, potentially enable anyone to take part in this research. Independent tests by people who are not committed to belief or disbelief in non-visual staring detection seem more likely to lead to an evidence-based consensus.

Control tests

Several commentators raised the possibility that the seemingly positive results in direct staring tests were a result of patterns in the randomizations combined with response biases or guessing strategies. Probably the best way to find out if these possible effects are important is to do control tests in which there is no staring at all. Possible artefacts should show up in the absence of a real effect. One method would be to deceive subjects into thinking that they are taking part in a regular experiment in which they are being looked at in staring trials, when in fact they are not. But this approach is ethically questionable.

Instead, I suggest doing control tests in which the subject is asked to guess in each trial whether the instructions are 'looking' or 'not looking', even though no staring takes place. The other participant sits with his or her back to the subject. The subject is given feedback as to whether the guesses are right or wrong. Artefacts that arise from any particular system of randomization, or from matching biases in the responses, or from implicit learning of possible randomization patterns should lead to hit rates above chance.

I have carried out some preliminary control tests using this procedure, working with subjects whose hit rates were significantly above chance in standard tests. In a total of 580 control trials, the average hit rate was 49%; by the sign method, the score was 12+ 15– and 1=. These results were not significantly different from chance.

An additional advantage of carrying out such controls is that they enable other psi hypotheses to be tested. The hit rates could conceivably be above chance levels if the subject picked up the instructions by telepathy, or by clairvoyance, or by precognition of the feedback. Precognition can be eliminated by omitting feedback. Telepathy can be ruled out in automated tests in which no other person is involved; the computer signals the beginning of each trial, and the subject records the guesses directly onto the computer.

Comparison of direct looking and CCTV tests

Research on staring detection has proceeded on two parallel tracks, direct looking with guessing, and CCTV trials with the measurement of electrodermal activity (EDA). As several commentators pointed out, the physiological measurement is likely to be more sensitive, and it would be interesting to know how subjects respond physiologically in the direct looking trials, and also to find out how well their EDA correlates with their guesses.

It is now possible to carry out remote staring trials online, with the subjects viewed through web cams and streaming video. The subjects' responses can be measured physiologically, and they can also enter their guesses directly onto the computer.

The sensitivity of different parts of the body

In standard looking trials, the starers focussed on the backs of the subjects' necks. These trials do not investigate whether subjects can tell which parts of their bodies are being stared at.

Nelson and Schwartz (2005) recently described a staring detection test in which the starer either focussed on the back of the subject's head or on the small of the back. The subject had to guess which area was being looked at. The average hit rate was 57%, significantly above the chance level of 50%. In standard yes/no staring detection trials, the same subjects' hit rate was 55%, similar to the hit rates in many other yes/no trials.

Can other researchers replicate this finding? If so, it opens a way to investigate the scopaesthetic sensitivity of different regions of the body, which would be easiest to study in pre-selected sensitive subjects. Can a sensitive subject distinguish between stares at the upper and lower back? What is the minimum distance that can be discriminated? Which regions of the body are most sensitive? The pattern of sensitivity could be mapped experimentally.

The natural history of scopaesthesia

As Ian Baker pointed out, surveillance through CCTV is now a common part of everyday life, and in that sense it is 'ecological'. However, almost no research has been done on people's sensitivity to this form of observation, and it would be good to find out more about it with the help of surveillance professionals and people who are unusually sensitive to being observed.

Fontana raised 'a whole raft of questions' about the way in which staring detection might work, and made the interesting suggestion that a combination of self-reports and autonomic reactions might help answer some of these questions. Martial arts practitioners might be good subjects for investigations of this kind.

Automated test procedures

The computerized 'eyes in the back of the head' test in the NeMo Centre in Amsterdam was set up in 1995, and more than 18,000 subject-looker pairs have taken part, as described in my first paper in this issue of *JCS*. Several other researchers, including Colwell *et al.* (2000) and Lobach and Bierman (2004), have also developed automated test procedures. The most sophisticated is that of Radin (2004), where the subjects, who are blindfolded, signal their guesses by pushing buttons on a 'gamepad' peripheral, normally used for playing video games.

I have already described my own online test (my paper 1). As Schmidt found, one technical question was whether or not participants should be able to change previous guesses. If they could, people might cheat by changing their guesses after they had received feedback. In order to block this possibility, participants were unable to alter the previous answer by pressing the 'Back' button. But then people who had made an honest mistake and wanted to correct it, like Schmidt, pushed the system into untested waters. Obviously this technical problem needs solving.

In an improved, second-generation online system, the computer would instruct the looker what to do, and at the same time, by means of a sound signal, alert both looker and subject that the test was beginning. There would still be a 'basic' option, where the subject tells the looker his or her guess, and the looker enters this into the computer. But there would also be a 'remote' option, in which the subject would have a mobile (cell) phone connected, through a dedicated telephone number, to the test website. The instructions to the subject, the signal for the beginning of each trial, and the guess would be communicated through the mobile phone. This system would enable staring trials to be conducted through windows, one-way mirrors, binoculars or CCTV, and also through web cams on the Internet. A recent technological advance allows EDA electrodes to be connected to mobile phones, so physiological measurements could also be carried out remotely.

Such an online system would enable any pair of people to test themselves. It would also enable college instructors and schoolteachers to set this test as an assignment to their classes, and to select sensitive subjects for further tests under more rigorous conditions.

If scopaesthesia turns out not to exist, the sceptical case will be strengthened, Blackmore's and Koch's dismissive attitude will be vindicated, and the conventional intromission paradigm will be reinforced. Research will then be needed to find out why the illusion of non-visual staring detection is so pervasive all over the world. But if non-visual staring detection does indeed occur, then a debate about possible explanations will be inevitable.

References

Colwell, J., Schröder, S. & Sladen, D. (2000), 'The ability to detect unseen staring: A literature review and empirical tests', *British Journal of Psychology*, **91**, pp. 71–85.

Gray, J. (2004), *Consciousness: Creeping Up On the Hard Problem* (Oxford: Oxford University Press).

Gregory, R.L. (1998), *Eye and Brain*, fifth edition (Oxford: Oxford University Press).

Lehar, S. (2003), 'Gestalt isomorphism and the primacy of subjective conscious experience: A gestalt bubble model', *Behavioral and Brain Sciences*, **26**, pp. 375–444.

Lobach, E. & Bierman, D.J. (2004), 'The invisible gaze: Three attempts to replicate Sheldrake's staring effects', *Proceedings of Parapsychology Association Annual Convention, 2004* (in press).

Nelson, L.A. and Schwartz, G.E. (2005), 'Human biofield and intention detection: Individual differences', *Journal of Alternative and Complementary Medicine*, **11**, pp. 93–101.

Parker, A. (2003), *In the Blink of an Eye: The Cause of the Most Dramatic Event in the History of Life* (London: The Free Press).

Pribram, K.H. (1991), *Brain and Perception* (Hillsdale, NJ: Lawrence Erlbaum Associates).

Radin, D. (2004), 'The feeling of being stared at: An analysis and replication'. *Journal of the Society for Psychical Research*, **68**, pp. 245–52.

Sheldrake, R. (1988), *The Presence of the Past: Morphic Resonance and the Habits of Nature* (London: Collins).

Sheldrake, R. (2003), *The Sense of Being Stared At, And Other Aspects of the Extended Mind* (London: Hutchinson).

JCS SUBSCRIPTION ORDER FORM

secure web ordering: www.imprint-academic.com/jcs

Name . . . .

Address * . . . .

. . . .

Home phone no . . . . Email . . . .

Credit card customers must supply cardholder registered address

ANNUAL SUBSCRIPTION RATES: Volume 12 (2005)

Twelve monthly issues. Prices include accelerated delivery (UK & USA), rest of world surface.

Individuals: $115/£62   Libraries: $385/£203   Students: $84/£46.50*
*(full-time student status evidence & course completion date required)
New for 2005: If you have a UK bank account you may like to consider subscribing by
Bankers' Direct Debit for only £15.00 per quarter. Contact sandra@imprint.co.uk for details.

❑ Please enter my library/individual/student subscription for Vol.12 ❑Airmail extra: $52/£26

Free with new subscription. Choose one of the following special back issues:
❑ *Trusting the Subject, Part 1* (10, No.9-10), ed. Jack & Roepstorff
❑ *Psi Wars: Getting to grips with the paranormal* (10, No.6-7), ed. J. Alcock *et al.*
❑ *Is the Visual World a Grand Illusion?* (9, No.5-6), ed. Alva Noë
❑ *The Varieties of Religious Experience: Centenary Essays* (9, No.9-10), ed. M. Ferrari
❑ *The View from Within: first person approaches* (6, No.2-3), ed. F.J.Varela & J.Shear
❑ *Reclaiming Cognition: action, intention & emotion* (6, No.11-12), ed. Freeman & Núñez
❑ *Between Ourselves: second-person approaches* (8, No.5-7), ed. Evan Thompson

Back Volumes Special Offer

The full set of back volumes 1–11 (1994–2004) @ *70% discount*. Includes all special issues.
Individuals and Students: $380/£205; Institutions: $1,270/£670.

❑ Please enter my Individual/Student/Institutional discount back volume order.

Payment Details

❑ Check — pay 'Imprint Academic' — $US (drawn on US bank or £ Sterling, drawn on UK)

❑ VISA ❑MASTERCARD ❑AMEX ❑SWITCH ❑DELTA ❑JCB

Card No . . . .

Expiry date . . . . . Signed . . . .
Credit cards (except US Amex) charged in £ Sterling and converted to local currency by card issuer

❑ **10% introductory discount on Volume 12 for CCDD (credit card direct debit)**,
whereby you authorise us to charge your card at annual subscription renewal time. We will notify you
by post in advance to give you plenty of time to cancel the transaction and your consumer rights are
fully protected by your card issuer. *I authorise Imprint Academic to recharge my card on the annual
subscription renewal date. Signed . . . .*

ORDER OFFICES:

US: Consciousness Studies, Dept. of Psychology, University of Arizona, Tucson AZ 85721
Rest of World: Imprint Academic, PO Box 200, Exeter EX5 5YX, UK
Tel: +44 (0)1392 841600 Fax: +44 (0)1392 841478 sandra@imprint.co.uk

Executive Editors

Joseph A. Goguen (Editor in Chief). Department of Computer Science
   University of California at San Diego, La Jolla, CA 92093-0114, USA.
   Phone: (858) 534-4197. Fax: (858) 534-7029. Email: goguen@cs.ucsd.edu

Robert K.C. Forman, Director, The Forge Institute,
   383 Broadway, Hastings on Hudson, NY 10706, USA.
   Tel/Fax: (914) 478 7802. Email: Forman@TheForge.org

Keith Sutherland (Publisher). Imprint Academic, PO Box 200, Exeter
   EX5 5YX, UK. Tel: +44 1392 841600 Email: keith@imprint.co.uk

Managing Editor *(address for manuscript submissions and books for review)*
Anthony Freeman, Imprint Academic, PO Box 200, Exeter EX5 5YX, UK.
   Tel: +44 1392 841600. Email: anthony@imprint.co.uk

Associate Editors

Jean *Burns*, 1525 – 153rd Avenue, San Leandro, CA 94578, USA.
   Tel: (510) 481 7507. Email: jeanbur@earthlink.net
Ivo Mosley (Poetry), Imprint Academic, PO Box 200, Exeter EX5 5YX, UK.
   Tel: +44 1392 841600. Email: ivomosley@aol.com
Chris Nunn (Book Reviews), Imprint Academic, PO Box 200, Exeter EX5
   5YX, UK. Tel: +44 1392 841600. Email: chrisnunn@compuserve.com
Jonathan Shear, Department of Philosophy, Virginia Commonwealth
   University, Richmond, VA 23284-2025, USA.
   Tel/Fax: (804) 282 2119. Email: jcs@infionline.net

Annual Subscription Rates (for 12 monthly issues)
Individuals: $115/£62
Institutions: $385/£203
Includes accelerated delivery (UK & USA), surface mail rest of world.
Orders to : Imprint Academic, PO Box 200, Exeter EX5 5YX, UK.
Tel: +44 1392 841600; Fax: 841478; Email: sandra@imprint.co.uk.
Cheques (£ or $US 'Imprint Academic'); VISA/AMEX/MASTERCARD

STYLE SHEET AND GUIDE TO AUTHORS

JCS is aimed at an educated multi-disciplinary readership. Authors should not assume prior knowledge in a subject speciality and should provide background information for their research. The use of technical terms should be avoided or made explicit. Where technical details are essential (for example in laboratory experiments), include them in footnotes or appendices, leaving the text accessible to the non-specialist reader. The same principle should also apply to non-essential mathematics.

Articles should not normally exceed 9,000 words (including footnotes). A short 150 word summary should accompany each submission. In general authors should adhere to the usages and conventions in Fowler's *Modern English Usage* which should be consulted for all questions not covered in these notes.

Footnote numbering should be consecutive superscript throughout the article. References to books and articles should be by way of author (date) or (author, date). Multiple publications from the same year should be labelled (Skinner, 1966a, b, c . . .). A single bibliography at the end should be compiled alphabetically observing the following conventions:

1 **References to complete books** should take the following form:
   Dennett, D.C. (1998), *Brainchildren* (Cambridge, MA: MIT Press).

2 **References to chapters in books** should take the following form:
   Wilkes, K. (1995), 'Losing consciousness', in *Conscious Experience*,
   ed. T. Metzinger (Paderborn: Schöningh).

3 **References to articles** should take the following form:
   Humphrey, N. (2000), 'How to solve the mind–body problem', *Journal of Consciousness Studies*, **7** (4), pp. 5–20.

SUBMISSION OF MANUSCRIPTS BY EMAIL

Authors are encouraged to email their wordprocessor files (retaining italics, accents, superscripts, footnotes etc.) or PDF files. We cannot currently review LaTex files. Send all submissions to **anthony@imprint.co.uk**.

Where it is necessary to send contributions by normal mail, they should be clearly typed in double spacing. One hard copy should be submitted, plus a copy of the article on disk. This will enable us to email it to editors and reviewers and speed up the review process. Please state what machine and wordprocessing program was used to prepare the text.